Those Wonderful Old Automobiles

Those Wonderful

Books by Floyd Clymer

FLOYD CLYMER

Old Automobiles

BONANZA BOOKS • NEW YORK

This edition published by BONANZA BOOKS,
a division of Crown Publishers, Inc.,
by arrangement with The McGraw-Hill Book Company, Inc.

VWXYZ

THOSE WONDERFUL OLD AUTOMOBILES

Copyright, 1953, by Floyd Clymer

Library of Congress Catalogue Card Number: 53-9010

Printed in the United States of America

THIS BOOK IS DEDICATED TO MY MOTHER

ELLA DUFF CLYMER

At the tender age of eleven when I was a Reo, Maxwell, and Cadillac dealer in Berthoud, Colorado, it was my mother who, together with my father, Dr. J. B. Clymer, a small-town physician, encouraged me in all my endeavors. She tolerated my lugging home all sorts of catalogs, pictures, newspapers, books, and magazines having to do with the early automobile, which I piled high in the attic, basement, my bedroom, and the garage (then called the "auto shed"). For her early encouragement I am forever thankful, for from all this accumulated material my Motorbooks years later got their start.

When I would walk into the house with greasy hands and smudged face, with oil on my clothes and reeking of the auto shed, it was always Mother who excused me first. Many times when Dad spoke sharply of my appearance Mother had a stock admonition for him: "Now, Joe, you started him on this auto business and you haven't any right to scold him now. Remember, you were a boy once yourself!" After that little admonition by Mother, Dad always kept quiet.

Preface

Those Wonderful Old Automobiles has been compiled in a vein of automobile nostalgia. This book is meant to be neither an analytical study nor a definitive history of the American automobile. In the pages that follow, I have attempted to convey my experience and feelings regarding early cars in America. It would be impossible for me, or anyone else, to cover fully every aspect of the history of American automobiles in a single volume—or in ten volumes, for that matter. However, the reader will find in the pages that follow a brief treatment of each of the pioneer automobile manufacturers still in business, as well as many historical notes about the little-known or short-lived cars of yesteryear.

I have lived close to automobiles all my life and have watched, at first hand, many of the important developments. This book is directed both to the younger generation which has not had that opportunity and to those of my contemporaries who wish to relive and recall the progress of the automobile in our times. If the reader finds a new or renewed appreciation of "those wonderful old automobiles" which played such a prominent role in promoting American industry and the high standard of living we now enjoy, the author will have accomplished his purpose.

FLOYD CLYMER

Acknowledgments

In compiling such a book as this, it becomes necessary to secure material from sources outside my own library. I therefore wish to thank the following persons and firms for their kind cooperation and assistance in supplying portions of the material included in this book:

Mrs. Gladys Olds Anderson; A. L. Beals; M. B. Berger; Herbert D. Brown; Walt Dibblee; George Dorris; Cornelius W. Hauck; Fred J. Lamborn; Jimmie Lynch; Ralph McCune; Albert Mecham; D. Cameron Peck; Homer E. Reid; Herbert Royston; Dr. R. E. Sayers; Charles B. Scoville, Jr.; Henry R. Selden; Hi Sibley; Major M. D. Stone; Pat Whittington.

Acme Newspictures, Inc.; The Autocar Company; Automobile Manufacturers Association; Batton, Barton, Durstine and Osborn, Inc.; Buick Motor Division, General Motors Corporation; Cadillac Motor Car Division, General Motors Corporation; Chevrolet Division, General Motors Corporation; Dodge Division, Chrysler Corporation; The Ethyl Corporation; Firestone Tire and Rubber Company; Ford Division, Ford Motor Company; GMC Truck and Coach Division, General Motors Corporation; Hudson Motor Car Company; Lincoln-Mercury Division, Ford Motor Company; Motor Truck Division, International Harvester Company; Nash Motors Division, Nash-Kelvinator Corporation; R. E. Olds Company; Oldsmobile Division, General Motors Corporation; Packard Motor Car Company; Plymouth Division, Chrysler Corporation; Pontiac Motor Division, General Motors Corporation; Reo Motors, Inc.; The Studebaker Corporation; Thompson Products, Inc.; Transportation Department, Twentieth Century-Fox Film Corporation; Trumbull Manufacturing Company; White Motor Company; Willys-Overland Motors, Inc.

Auto Pioneering (Story of R. E. Olds) by Duane Yarnell; *Esquire* magazine (for permission to reproduce Peter Helck's paintings); *True* magazine (for permission to reproduce Peter Helck's paintings).

Long Island Automotive Museum, Southampton, Long Island, New York; Museum of Antique Autos, Princeton, Massachusetts; Museum of Science and Industry, Chicago, Illinois; The Smithsonian Institution, Washington, D.C.; The Thompson Museum, Cleveland, Ohio.

Foreword

The instinctive drive in the American character is to replace what we have today with a more advanced model tomorrow. This headlong surge to progress keeps our eyes so focused on the next step ahead that we seldom spare even a glimpse at the steps of the past that brought us to where we are today.

First, in the *Treasury of Early American Automobiles*, and now in *Those Wonderful Old Automobiles*, Floyd Clymer has given us a veritable museum of nostalgic memories for the days when motoring was an adventure as well as a family outing.

But there is much more represented in these books than just a love of nostalgia. For behind the story of the automobile, from its birth to its present status in our way of life, is the story of America's mass production and mastery of the machine.

In my generation the automobile fired the imagination of youngsters. I fell in love with the horseless carriage in a Columbus, Ohio, garage where the boss let me alternate between sweeping out the machine shop and tinkering with a Waverly Electric, a one-cylinder Oldsmobile, and a steam Locomobile.

My story is by no means unique. Thousands of others started with the automobile and, like myself, branched off into other lines of endeavor where a keen interest in machinery and its operation was a prerequisite to success.

Beginning with 1900, American manufacturers will probably have turned out, by the end of 1953, some 100,000,000 automobiles and trucks with a total value of nearly $100,000,000,000. But, even in dollars and cents, this is just a fraction of the industry's contribution to our economy. The actual wealth contributed to our nation by the many direct by-products of the automobile, such as highway construction, gasoline and oil refining, and tire manufacturing, is staggering.

Still behind all these things is the know-how that came out of remote garages as auto pioneers assembled those "horseless" carriages. That know-how not only has enabled us to turn out planes and tanks and guns to insure our security through two global wars, but it has built for us thousands of appliances which have emancipated us from drudgery and made life more enjoyable for us all.

Floyd Clymer's books accomplish two great purposes. They are an everlasting monument to the men who struggled and suffered untold heartbreak to build the world's greatest industry. In addition, they will be an inspiration to the younger generations. They demonstrate, above all, that under our free enterprise system perseverance, common sense, and hard work on the part of individuals can carry a mere idea from humble beginnings to a constructive force that can change and enrich an entire civilization.

CAPTAIN EDDIE RICKENBACKER
PRESIDENT AND GENERAL MANAGER
Eastern Air Lines, Inc.

Contents

I. Transport without the Horse

Three-wheelers

Before 1900, when the automotive industry was in swaddling clothes, inventors and designers were not exactly sure whether a three- or four-wheeled automobile would be the more satisfactory. Here are several types of the earliest three-wheel vehicles. Below is a British powered tricycle which was exhibited at a London show in the 1880s. It appears to be driven by a 2-cylinder compressed-air engine. There is a large hand pump at the rear near two wicker-bound air reservoirs.

At top right is a steam car manufactured in 1896 by M. Palmesoole Groote Stevoort, of Belgium. This contraption had a bicycle-type front wheel controlled by steering arms, wire wheels with solid tires, and full elliptic rear springs. In 1897 the inventor decided that front-wheel drive would improve the performance of the car, and installed a top to protect the driver (middle, right). But by 1899 M. Stevoort had made real progress. He discarded the wire wheels, and the car was again driven by the rear wheels, with an extremely large single drive chain. A step was mounted for the convenience of driver and passenger, and operating levers were fixed in the center of the floorboard. The seat was upholstered, and fenders offered the occupants a modicum of protection. The steering device was of a folding design. (Photo at bottom, right.)

Earliest Development

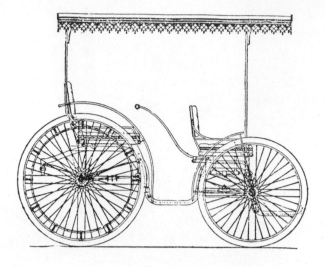

Today most people are under the illusion that the horseless-carriage age started at the turn of the century, but actually there was a great deal of important activity in the nineties and even before. Henry Ford tinkered with his first buggy in 1894; Ransom E. Olds produced his first gas-driven car in 1897; and Alexander Winton built one in 1895. Late in the nineteenth century a number of imaginative inventors were tinkering with many types of horseless carriages. At left is an electric car designed by B. J. Arnold, then a prominent electrical engineer. He intended it for "boulevard service" and, since he was an expert designer of traction engines, Mr. Arnold introduced some novel features in the transmission and compensating gear. The batteries were placed under the body of what he called an "electric wagon." The steering lever was operated from the back seat. It was common practice in early days for the passengers to ride in the front seat. Solid rubber wire-spoked wheels were used; the stationary canopy top could not be lowered but could be removed.

Left: In 1899 the Benz Company, of Germany, built a new luxury car called "Mylord." Note the unusual levers mounted alongside the right of the front seat. A double chain drive, very popular at that time, was used. Since this was before the days when pneumatic tires came into general use, this car had wooden spokes and solid rubber tires.

At lower left is a light car, the Electromobile, introduced in October, 1899, by the Belknap Company. Many bicycle parts were used in the design. It appears that the body was mounted between odd-looking bicycle frames with bicycle forks and rear sections also used. This mysterious illustration does not show how the driver steered the car, but it may be that the steering mechanism was operated by a foot control, as the two front bicycle-fork sections are connected at the top of the fork stems.

Electrics

Around 1900 the automobile's future was confused. Would electric, steam, or gasoline vehicles dominate? One of the earliest and best-known electric cars was the Waverley. The advertisement below stated it was "not only light and safe, [but] noiseless, odorless, clean, durable, comfortable, and simple in operation." What manufacturer of modern cars can claim as much today?

Below, right, is another popular early electric car, made by the Woods Motor Vehicle Company. This 1900 ad features the "Spider" model. The enthusiastic writer claimed that the effective twentieth-century vehicle such as the Woods was "not only noiseless and odorless, [but] free from danger." He also advised the prospect that there was no use waiting for lower prices or improvements; apparently he thought this car was the acme of perfection. The Woods was designed for the carriage trade, as it was operated by a chauffeur seated high behind the passengers. This fortunate fellow in the top hat was monarch of all he surveyed, with an excellent view of the road from his high perch.

Waverley *Electromobile*

Model 18. $1000.

A new departure in electric vehicle construction; light, safe, noiseless, odorless, clean, durable, comfortable, simple in operation. Battery guaranteed for two years. In no other vehicle are all these desirable qualities combined.

Wheels, thirty-four inches
Tires, one and five-eighths inches, solid rubber
Speed, three to sixteen miles per hour
Height of body from ground, twenty-seven inches

We can make prompt shipment of this model. Reliable agents wanted in unoccupied territory. Catalogue illustrating 18 models for two 2c. stamps.

AMERICAN BICYCLE COMPANY

Waverley Factory, Indianapolis, Ind.

NEW YORK SALESROOM - - - 943 EIGHTH AVENUE

"SPIDER"

DON'T WAIT
FOR LOWER PRICES OR "IMPROVEMENTS"!

THE WOODS ELECTRICS to-day are reasonable in price, and thoroughly effective 20th-Century Automobiles—noiseless, odorless, free from danger. Their method of construction cannot be surpassed and the workmanship and material are of the finest quality.

Our Illustrated Booklet will be sent on request.

WOODS MOTOR VEHICLE CO.

NEW YORK;   CHICAGO;
44th St. and Vanderbilt Ave.   545-549 Wabash Ave.

Assemble Your Own, 1903

The industry had started to expand by 1903 when the Brecht Automobile Company (below, left) of St. Louis offered to supply two different styles of running gears (chassis) so the purchaser could assemble his own car, electric, steam, or gas. Furthermore, it offered either solid or pneumatic tires and the chassis was complete with springs and wood wheels. Several early manufacturers offered automobiles in knockdown form.

Below, right, is the Scott car, manufactured in St. Louis by the makers of Reliable storage batteries. Note the claim of "30 miles on one battery charge," which was quite a remarkable feat and well worth talking about then.

Below is the $800 Northern Runabout, also a 1903 model, which was one of the first cars to be manufactured in Detroit. In some ways this little car was similar to the famous curved-dash Oldsmobile, in that it had a single-cylinder engine mounted in the rear and the car could be cranked from the driver's seat. Wood artillery wheels were used and the brake drum and band were housed within the center differential unit. The Northern had two forward speeds and one reverse.

Horseless Carriage with Whip

In 1900, the census reported that there were some 76,000,000 people living in the United States and fewer than 4,000 of these were car owners. As we look back at car prices in those pre-inflation days, they seem very low indeed to us today, but, in fact, the automobile was too expensive for all save a very few families. Wages were low, farm prices were lower, and $100 in cash was, psychologically and actually, a great deal of money. Nevertheless, the automobile industry needed to tap only a very small percentage of these 76,000,000 potential buyers to reap rich rewards. If the auto maker could reach approximately 3 of every 10,000 families, he could sell all the cars he could make.

The chap at right might have been the Henry Ford of the South. He is Gilbert Waters, of New Bern, North Carolina. He found the public too skeptical at the turn of the century to finance his automobile venture, so he went back to his machine shop instead of becoming a manufacturer of horseless carriages. Mounted on the steering lever is a bicycle bell, and a whip extends from the whip socket at his left.

Below are two models of the 1904 Crestmobile, once manufactured in Cambridge, Massachusetts. This small car had an 8-horsepower engine and weighed less than 1,000 pounds. It was one of the earlier shaft-driven cars. The makers claimed that the air-cooled gasoline engine worked perfectly and had little vibration.

Model D.
$900.00 for four persons. $800.00 for two persons.

Delivery Wagon. $900.00.

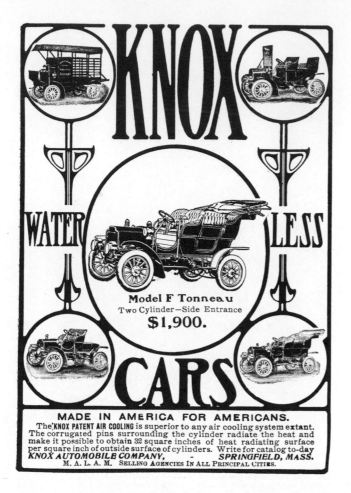

MADE IN AMERICA FOR AMERICANS.

The KNOX PATENT AIR COOLING is superior to any air cooling system extant. The corrugated pins surrounding the cylinder radiate the heat and make it possible to obtain 32 square inches of heat radiating surface per square inch of outside surface of cylinders. Write for catalog to-day

KNOX AUTOMOBILE COMPANY,   -   SPRINGFIELD, MASS.

M. A. L. A. M. Selling Agencies In All Principal Cities.

At left are shown various models of the 1906 Waterless Knox manufactured in Springfield, Massachusetts. The Knox had a unique arrangement for air cooling in that a large number of corrugated pins were welded to the cylinder. Claims were made that they radiated the heat and made it possible to obtain 32 square inches of heat-radiating surface per square inch of outside surface of cylinder. The Knox Company in later years manufactured water-cooled cars and abandoned air cooling.

Below, left, is a 1905 ad of the Brooklyn Automobile Company, who were agents for Haynes-Apperson cars. This touring car had a canopy top and was acclaimed, by the manufacturers, as "the most handsome car on the American market built for American roads." This may have been a slap at the influx of foreign makes which were even then finding some degree of popularity in the United States. The small two-passenger car had the driver on the left-hand side, which showed some degree of foresight. The single gas headlight is located in the center. Below, right, is a famous early American model, the Royal Tourist, manufactured in Cleveland.

$3,000

32-38 horse power, 2,500 pounds, 4 cylinders, vertical, shaft drive. More Exclusive Features of Merit than any other car in America. Guaranteed Deliveries. Write Dept. M for catalog.

ROYAL MOTOR CAR CO.   -   Cleveland, Ohio

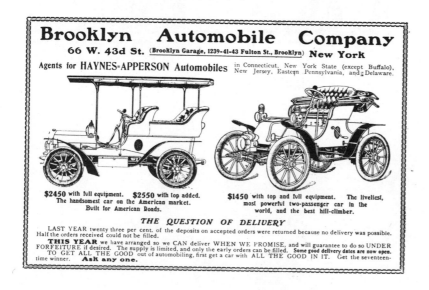

Brooklyn   Automobile   Company

66 W. 43d St. (Brooklyn Garage, 1239-41-43 Fulton St., Brooklyn) New York

Agents for HAYNES-APPERSON Automobiles in Connecticut, New York State (except Buffalo), New Jersey, Eastern Pennsylvania, and Delaware.

$2450 with full equipment. $2550 with top added.
The handsomest car on the American market.
Built for American Roads.

$1450 with top and full equipment.   The liveliest, most powerful two-passenger car in the world, and the best hill-climber.

THE QUESTION OF DELIVERY

LAST YEAR twenty three per cent. of the deposits on accepted orders were returned because no delivery was possible. Half the orders received could not be filled.

THIS YEAR we have arranged so we CAN deliver WHEN WE PROMISE, and will guarantee to do so UNDER FORFEITURE if desired. The supply is limited, and only the early orders can be filled. Some good delivery dates are now open. TO GET ALL THE GOOD out of automobiling, first get a car with ALL THE GOOD IN IT. Get the seventeen-time winner. **Ask any one.**

A Pioneer Company

One of the pioneer mechanical firms of America, established in 1850 and celebrating a century of service in 1950, is the Trumbull Manufacturing Company of Warren, Ohio. Operating under various names before 1874 (the original name of the firm was the Warren Machine Works), the present company has had an interesting history. At one time it was in the automobile business and manufactured the first Trumbull car in 1899 (top, right). It was a single-cylinder runabout with the engine at the rear and was equipped with full elliptic rear springs. The passengers rode in front and there was a folding top.

Later, in 1902, the company manufactured the plush five-passenger touring car at right with a water-cooled engine, wood artillery wheels, and clincher tires. In 1905 Trumbull manufactured a car called the Pendleton (shown below, right), with a folding steering wheel which made it easier for the driver to get in and out of the car.

The speed with which the automobile business developed in this country is indicated by this sketch (below) from a copy of *Popular Mechanics* magazine of 1909. Only ten years after the first Trumbull made its appearance, two cars were traveling daily between San Angelo and Big Springs, Texas, a distance of 100 miles, carrying both passengers and mail.

Franklin "Air Cooling," 1906

H. H. Franklin was a pioneer builder of motor-cars and throughout the years manufactured nothing but air-cooled automobiles. Most popular Franklins were the four- and six-cylinder models, which had full elliptic springs and wooden frames. Light weight was always a Franklin talking point. The case for air cooling is ably presented below.

FRANKLIN

Type G Four-cylinder Light Touring-car. Shaft Drive. 1400 pounds. $1800.

How does "Franklin air-cooling" make a more powerful engine, and an abler car for less money?

By creating a more efficient temperature in the combustion chambers than is possible in any other engine. By also getting rid of weight. By saving repair-cost and weight-cost; and by giving more days' work in a year.

The Franklin auxiliary exhaust does what no other invention ever did for a motor-car cylinder; lets out the hot, used gases before they have a chance to over-heat the cylinder. It prevents flame being carried out along the main valves to burn or pit them, and cause them to leak compression. It permits the cylinders, being cooler, to take in a larger charge, and enables the charge to do its full work freely and unhampered.

And here is an equally important fact; while Franklin cylinders do not over-heat, they also do not under-heat. A certain degree of constant heat is necessary for the best work in a gas-motor cylinder. Franklin direct air-cooling creates exactly the most efficient working temperature in the cylinder, while the Franklin auxiliary exhaust maintains this temperature constantly.

Thus the Franklin engine yields its full ability from the start, and keeps it up continuously—produces big power, saves a large percentage of the power that is lost in standard cylinders, and delivers to the Franklin rear wheels an exceptional amount of active working energy.

The weight of water-cooling apparatus—pipes, pumps, tanks, radiator, water; and the heavier frame needed to carry them—a total of some 200 useless pounds—are all dispensed with; and the power left free to carry people; and to go.

No water-cooling repairs are needed. Fuel and oil bills are small because of light weight and reduced friction. The light weight makes an enormous saving on tires.

There's nothing to freeze. A Franklin car is ready for use any minute, in any climate—365 days in the year. That brings down the cost for every day's use.

Send for the handsomest and clearest of all motor-car catalogues.

4 Models for 1906

4-cylinder Runabout, $1400. 4-cylinder Touring-car, $2800.
4-cylinder Light Touring-car, $1800. 6-cylinder Touring-car, $4000.
Prices f. o. b. Syracuse, N. Y.

H. H. FRANKLIN MFG. CO., Syracuse, N. Y., *M. A. L. A. M.*

Motorcars of 1906

Here is a list that is supposed to include all of the automobiles manufactured in 1906. It was published by *Cosmopolitan* magazine as a directory for three national motor shows as well as several local shows, but it was stated that a number of the cars would not be shown that year.

This list includes valuable technical information as well as the price and the place of manufacture. Even as early as 1906, the industry began to gravitate toward Michigan, although a number of makes were built in Indiana, Ohio, and other states.

THE 1906 MOTOR-CAR DIRECTORY

Gasoline Motor-Cars

Orient, 4 h. p. buckboard; Waltham Mfg. Co., Waltham, Mass.
Price, $400; seats 2 persons; single, air-cooled cylinder; dry battery ignition; transmission, friction; speeds, forward and reverse; weight, 600 pounds.

Ford, 15 h. p.; Ford Motor Co., Detroit, Mich.
Price, $450; seats 2 persons; 4 water-cooled, vertical cylinders; dry battery ignition; planetary transmission; 2 speeds; weight, 700 pounds.

Monarch, 7½ h. p.; Joseph S. Heller, New York, N. Y.
Price, $500; seats 2 persons; single, horizontal, air-cooled cylinder; jump spark ignition; planetary transmission; 3 speeds; weight, 900 pounds.

Walker, Walker Motor Car Co., Detroit, Mich.
Price, $550; seats 2 persons; 2 water-cooled, opposed cylinders; jump spark ignition; planetary transmission; 3 speeds; weight, 600 pounds.

Gale, 8 h. p.; Western Tool Works, Galesburg, Ill.
Price, $600; seats 2 persons; single, horizontal, water-cooled cylinder; jump spark ignition; spur gear transmission; 3 speeds; weight, 1,100 pounds.

Oldsmobile, 7 h. p.; Olds Motor Works, Lansing, Mich.
Price, $650; seats 2 persons; single, horizontal, water-cooled cylinder; jump spark ignition; planetary transmission; 3 speeds; weight, 1,100 pounds.

Northern, 7 h. p.; Northern Mfg. Co., Detroit, Mich.
Price, $650; seats 4 persons; single, horizontal, water-cooled cylinder; jump spark and battery ignition; planetary ignition; 3 speeds; weight, 1,100 pounds.

Gale, 8 h. p.; Western Tool Works, Galesburg, Ill.
Price, $650; seats 2 persons; single, horizontal, water-cooled cylinder; jump spark ignition; spur gear transmission; 3 speeds; weight, 1,100 pounds.

Reo, 8 h. p.; Reo Motor Car Co., Lansing, Mich.
Price, $650; seats 2 persons; single, horizontal, water-cooled cylinder; jump spark and dry battery ignition; planetary ignition; 3 speeds; weight 950 pounds.

Holsman, 10 h. p.; Holsman Automobile Co., Chicago, Ill.
Price, $650; seats 2 persons; 2 horizontal-opposed, air-cooled cylinders; jump spark ignition; steel cable transmission; weight, 800 pounds.

Wolverine; Wolverine Automobile and Commercial Vehicle Co., Dundee, Mich.
Price, $750; seats 2 persons; 2 water-cooled cylinders; jump spark ignition; planetary transmission; 3 speeds; weight, 1,000 pounds.

Reo, 8 h. p.; Reo Motor Car Co., Lansing, Mich.
Price, $675; seats 4 persons; single, horizontal, water-cooled cylinder; jump spark ignition; planetary transmission; 3 speeds; weight, 975 pounds.

Cadillac, 10 h. p.; Cadillac Motor Car Co., Detroit, Mich.
Price, $750; seats 2 persons; single, water-cooled cylinder; planetary transmission; 3 speeds; weight, 1,100 pounds.

Pierce, 12 h. p.; Pierce Engine Co., Racine Jct., Wis.
Price, $750; seats 2 persons; twin cylinder, water-cooled.

Maxwell, 10 h. p.; Maxwell-Briscoe Motor Co., Tarrytown, N. Y.
Price, $780; seats 2 persons; 2 double-opposed, water-cooled cylinders; jump spark ignition; planetary transmission; 3 speeds; weight, 1,000 pounds.

Stoddard-Dayton, 15-18 h. p.; Dayton Motor Car Co., Dayton, Ohio.
Seats 2 persons; 4 twin, water-cooled cylinders; jump spark transmission; selective transmission; 4 speeds; weight, 1,200 pounds.

Wayne, 14 h. p.; Wayne Automobile Co., Detroit, Mich.
Price, $800; seats 2 persons; 2 opposed, water-cooled cylinders; jump spark ignition; planetary transmission; 3 speeds; weight, 975 pounds.

Holsman, 10 h. p.; Holsman Automobile Co., Chicago, Ill.
Price, $800; seats 4 persons; 2 horizontal-opposed, air-cooled cylinders; jump spark ignition; steel cable transmission; weight, 900 pounds.

Logan, 10 h. p.; Logan Const'n Co., Chillicothe, O.
Price, $900; seats 2 persons; 2 opposed, air-cooled cylinders; jump spark ignition; sliding gear transmission; 3 speeds; weight, 900 pounds.

Lambert, 16 h. p.; Buckeye Mfg. Co., Anderson, Ind.
Price, $900; seats 2 persons; 2 opposed, water-cooled cylinders; jump spark ignition; friction drive transmission; weight, 1,600 pounds.

Pierce, 8 h. p.; George N. Pierce Co., Buffalo, N. Y.
Price, $900, without top; seats 4 persons; single, water-cooled cylinder; jump spark ignition; planetary transmission; 3 speeds; weight, 1,250 pounds.

Model, 16-18 h. p.; Model Gas Engine Works, Auburn, Ind.
Price, $900; seats 2 persons; double-opposed, water-cooled cylinders; planetary or sliding gear transmission; 3 speeds; weight, 1,300 pounds.

The Kansas City Car

Not a New Product—but the development of six years of practical experience in car building

1906

The Car that Climbs the Hills

This car is fitted with 35 h. p. opposed motor, has two speeds forward and one reverse. Long wheel base, platform springs and built substantially and artistic indetail. Any make of tire.

Cadillac, 10 h. p. victoria; Cadillac Motor Car Co., Detroit, Mich.
Price, $950; seats 4 persons; single, water-cooled cylinder; jump spark ignition; planetary transmission; 3 speeds; weight, 1350 pounds.

Moline, 16 h. p.; Moline Automobile Co., East Moline, Ill.
Price, $1000; seats 4 persons; 2 horizontal-opposed, water-cooled cylinders; jump spark ignition; planetary transmission; 3 speeds; weight, 1100 pounds.

Ford, touring car; Ford Motor Co., Detroit, Mich.
Price, $1000; seats 5 persons; 2 horizontal-opposed, water-cooled cylinders; jump spark ignition; planetary transmission; 3 speeds; weight, 1400 pounds.

Autocar, 12-14 h. p.; The Autocar Company, Ardmore, Pa.
Price, $1000; seats 2 persons; 2 horizontal-opposed, water-cooled cylinders; jump spark ignition; sliding gear transmission; 4 speeds; weight, 1340 pounds.

Mitchell, 14-18 h. p.; Mitchell Motor Car Co., Racine Junction, Wis.
Price, $1000; seats 2 persons; 4 vertical, water-cooled cylinders; jump spark ignition; sliding gear transmission; 4 speeds; weight, 1200 pounds.

Buick, 22 h. p.; Buick Motor Co., Jackson, Mich.
Price, $1000; seats 2 persons; 2 double-opposed, water-cooled cylinders; jump spark ignition; spur gear transmission; 3 speeds; weight, 1200 pounds.

Cadillac, 10 h. p.; Cadillac Motor Car Co., Detroit, Mich.
Price, $1000; seats 4 persons; single, water-cooled cylinder; jump spark ignition; planetary transmission; 3 speeds; weight, 1350 pounds.

Zent, 14 h. p.; The Zent Automobile Co., Bellefontaine, O.
Price, $1000; seats 2 persons; 2 horizontal-opposed, air-cooled cylinders; jump spark ignition; planetary transmission; 3 speeds; weight, 900 pounds.

Lambert, 16 h. p.; The Buckeye Mfg. Co., Anderson, Ind.
Price, $1050; seats 5 persons; 2 opposed, water-cooled cylinders; jump spark ignition; friction drive transmission; weight, 1800 pounds.

Model, 24 h. p.; Model Gas Engine Works, Auburn, Ind.
Price, $1050; seats 5 persons; double opposed, water-cooled cylinders; planetary transmission; 3 speeds; weight, 1600 pounds.

Queen, 18 h. p.; The C. H. Blomstrom Motor Co., Detroit, Mich.
Price, $1100; seats 5 persons; 2 horizontal-opposed, water-cooled cylinders; jump spark ignition; planetary transmission; 3 speeds; weight, 1600 pounds.

Model, 16-18 h. p.; Model Gas Engine Works, Auburn, Ind.
Price, $1150; seats 5 persons; double-opposed, water-cooled cylinders; planetary or sliding gear transmission; 3 speeds; weight, 1420 pounds.

Pierce Racine, 18 h. p.; Pierce Engine Co., Racine Junction, Wis.
Price, $1150; seats 5 persons; 4 water-cooled cylinders.

1906 Ford 6 Cylinder Touring Car
Price $2,500

Michigan, 16 h. p.; Michigan Automobile Co., Ltd., Kalamazoo, Mich.
Price, $1200; seats 5 persons; 2 horizontal, water-cooled cylinders; jump spark ignition; planetary transmission; 3 speeds; weight, 1800 pounds.

Duryea, 3-wheeled phæton; Duryea Power Co., Reading, Pa.
Price, $1200; seats 2 adults and 2 children; 3 water-cooled cylinders; make-and-break spark ignition; planetary transmission; 3 speeds; weight, 950 pounds.

Lambert, 18 h. p.; The Buckeye Mfg. Co., Anderson, Ind.
Price, $1200; seats 5 persons; 2 opposed, water-cooled cylinders; jump spark ignition; friction drive; weight, 1800 pounds.

Rambler, 18 h. p.; Thomas B. Jeffery & Co., Kenosha, Wis.
Price, $1200; seats 5 persons; 2 horizontal-opposed, water-cooled cylinders; jump spark ignition; planetary transmission; 3 speeds.

Cadillac, 16 h. p. coupe; Cadillac Motor Car Co., Detroit, Mich.
Price, $1200; seats 2 persons; single, water-cooled cylinder; jump spark ignition; planetary transmission; 3 speeds.

Pierce Racine, 18 h. p.; Pierce Engine Co., Racine, Wis.
Price, $1250; seats 5 persons; 4 vertical cylinders; jump spark ignition; planetary transmission; 3 speeds; weight, 1400 pounds.

Oldsmobile, 24 h. p.; Olds Motor Works, Lansing, Mich.
Price, $1250; seats 4 persons; 2 vertical, water-cooled cylinders; jump spark ignition; sliding gear transmission; 4 speeds; weight, 1700 pounds.

Maxwell, 16-20 h. p.; Maxwell-Briscoe Co., Tarrytown, N. Y.
Price, $1250; seats 4 persons; double-opposed, water-cooled cylinders; jump spark ignition; sliding gear transmission; 4 speeds; weight, 1400 pounds.

Glide, 16-18 h. p.; Bartholomew Co., Peoria, Ill.
Price, $1250; seats 4 persons; horizontal double-opposed, water-cooled cylinders; jump spark ignition; planetary transmission; 3 speeds; weight, 1600 pounds.

Auburn, 20 h. p.; Auburn Automobile Co., Auburn, Ind.
Price, $1250; seats 5 persons; 2 water-cooled cylinders; jump spark ignition; planetary transmission; 3 speeds; weight, 1750 pounds.

Jackson, 20-24 h. p.; Jackson Automobile Co., Jackson, Mich.
Price, $1250; seats 5 persons; 2 horizontal-opposed, water-cooled cylinders; jump spark ignition; planetary transmission; 3 speeds; weight, 1750 pounds.

Wayne, 20 h. p.; Wayne Automobile Co., Detroit, Mich.
Price, $1250; seats 5 persons; 2 water-cooled cylinders; jump spark ignition; planetary transmission; 3 speeds; weight, 1600 pounds.

Reo, 16 h. p.; Reo Motor Car Co., Lansing, Mich.
Price, $1250; seats 5 persons; 2 horizontal-opposed, water-cooled cylinders; jump spark ignition; planetary transmission; 3 speeds; weight, 1000 pounds.

Dolson, 20 h. p.; Dolson Automobile Co., Charlotte, Mich.
Price, $1250; seats 5 persons; 2 horizontal, water-cooled cylinders; jump spark ignition; planetary transmission; 3 speeds; weight, 2000 pounds.

Gale, 18 h. p.; Western Tool Works, Galesburg, Ill.
Price, $1250; seats 5 persons; horizontal, double-opposed, water-cooled cylinders; jump spark ignition; spur gear transmission; 3 speeds; weight, 1700 pounds.

Model, 24 h. p.; Model Gas Engine Works, Auburn, Ind.
Price, $1250; seats 5 persons; double-opposed, water-cooled cylinders; planetary transmission; 3 speeds; weight, 1600 pounds.

Buick, 22 h. p.; Buick Motor Co., Jackson, Mich.
Price, $1250; seats 5 persons; double-opposed, water-cooled cylinders; jump spark ignition; spur gear transmission; 3 speeds; weight, 1800 pounds.

Stevens-Duryea, 7 h. p.; J. Stevens Arms & Tool Co., Chicopee Falls, Mass.
Price, $1300 with top; seats 4 persons; 2 horizontal, water-cooled cylinders; jump spark ignition; individual clutch transmission; 4 speeds; weight, 1350 pounds.

Duryea, 12-15 h. p.; Duryea Power Co., Reading, Pa.
Price, $1300; seats 2 adults and 2 children; 3 water-cooled cylinders; make-and-break magneto ignition; planetary transmission; 3 speeds; weight, 1050 pounds.

Rambler, 20 h. p.; Thomas B. Jeffery & Co., Kenosha, Wis.
Price, $1350; seats 5 persons; 2 horizontal-opposed, water-cooled cylinders; jump spark ignition; planetary transmission; 3 speeds.

Gale, 18 h. p.; Western Tool Works, Galesburg, Ill.
Price, $1350; seats 5 persons; horizontal, double-opposed, water-cooled cylinders; jump spark ignition; spur gear transmission; 3 speeds; weight, 1700 pounds.

Franklin, 12 h. p.; H. H. Franklin Mfg. Co., Syracuse, N. Y.
Price, $1400; seats 2 persons; 4 vertical, air-cooled cylinders; jump spark ignition; planetary transmission; 3 speeds; weight, 1100 pounds.

Stanhope, 15 h. p.; Twyford Motor Car Co., Brookville, Pa.
Price, $1400; seats 4 persons; 2 upright, water-cooled cylinders; jump spark ignition; weight, 1300 pounds.

Compound, 12-15 h. p.; E. H. V. Company, Middletown, Conn.
Price, $1400; seats 2 persons; 3 vertical, water-cooled cylinders; jump spark ignition; sliding gear transmission; 4 speeds; weight, 1400 pounds.

Knox, 14-16 h. p.; Knox Automobile Company, Springfield, Mass.
Price, $1400; seats 2 persons; 2 horizontal, air-cooled cylinders; jump spark ignition; planetary transmission; 3 speeds; weight, 1600 pounds.

Compound, 12-15 h. p.; E. H. V. Company, Middletown, Conn.
Price, $1400; seats 5 persons; 3 vertical, water-cooled cylinders; jump spark ignition; sliding gear transmission; 4 speeds; weight, 1650 pounds.

Maxwell, 16 h. p.; Maxwell-Briscoe Motor Co., Tarrytown, N. Y.
Price, $1450; seats 5 persons; 2 double-opposed, water-cooled cylinders; jump spark ignition; sliding gear transmission; 4 speeds; weight, 1600 pounds.

Dolson, 20 h. p.; Dolson Automobile Co., Charlotte, Mich.
Price, $1500; seats 5 persons; 2 opposed, water-cooled cylinders; dry cell ignition; sliding pinion transmission; 4 speeds; weight, 1750 pounds.

Marion, 16 h. p.; The Marion Motor Car Co., Indianapolis, Ind.
Price, $1500; seats 5 persons; 4 transverse, air-cooled cylinders; jump spark ignition; planetary transmission; 3 speeds; weight, 1750 pounds.

Jackson, 20-24 h. p.; Jackson Automobile Co., Jackson, Mich.
Price, $1500; seats 5 persons; 2 water-cooled cylinders; jump spark ignition; planetary transmission; 3 speeds; weight, 1900 pounds.

Premier, 16 h. p.; Premier Motor Mfg. Co., Indianapolis, Ind.
Price, $1500; seats 5 persons; 4 vertical air-cooled cylinders; jump spark ignition; planetary transmission; 3 speeds; weight, 1900 pounds.

Duryea, 12-15 h. p.; Duryea Power Co., Reading, Pa.
Price, $1500; seats 4 adults and 2 children; 3 water-cooled cylinders; make-and-break spark ignition; planetary transmission; 3 speeds; weight, 1150 pounds.

Lambert, 18 h. p.; Buckeye Mfg. Co., Anderson, Ind.
Price, $1500; seats 5 persons; 2 opposed, water-cooled cylinders; jump spark ignition; friction drive transmission; weight, 1800 pounds.

Knox, 14-16 h. p.; Knox Automobile Company, Springfield, Mass.
Price, $1500; seats 2 or 4 persons; 2 horizontal, air-cooled cylinders; jump spark ignition; 3 speeds; weight, 1850 pounds.

Oxford, 16 h. p.; Detroit-Oxford Mfg. Co., Oxford, Mich.
Price, $1500; seats 5 persons; 2 horizontal-opposed, water-cooled cylinders; jump spark ignition; direct drive transmission; 3 speeds; weight, 1500 pounds.

Elmore, 24 h. p.; Elmore Mfg. Co., Clyde, O.
2-cycle, vertical, water-cooled cylinders; roller contact ignition; planetary transmission; 3 speeds; weight, 1750 pounds.

Orient, 16 h. p.; Waltham Mfg. Co., Waltham, Mass.
Price, $1600; seats 2 persons; 4 air-cooled cylinders; jump spark ignition; sliding gear transmission; 4 speeds; weight, 1300 pounds.

Pope-Hartford, 8 h. p.; Pope Mfg. Co., Hartford, Conn.
Price, $1600; seats 5 persons; 2 horizontal-opposed, water-cooled cylinders; jump spark ignition; sliding gear transmission; 4 speeds; weight, 1800 pounds.

Rambler, 20 h. p. surrey; Thomas B. Jeffery & Co., Kenosha, Wis.
Price, $1650; seats 5 persons; 2 horizontal-opposed, water-cooled cylinders; jump spark ignition; planetary transmission; 3 speeds.

Cannon; Burt Mfg. Co., Kalamazoo, Mich.
Price, $1650; seats 4 persons; horizontal-opposed, water-cooled cylinders; jump spark ignition; friction transmission; 4 speeds; weight, 1650 pounds.

Columbia, 18-19 h. p.; Electric Vehicle Co., Hartford, Conn.
Price, $1750; seats 5 persons; 2 horizontal-opposed, water-cooled cylinders; jump spark ignition; sliding gear transmission; 4 speeds; weight, 1800 pounds.

Pierce Racine, 24 h. p.; Pierce Engine Co., Racine, Junction, Wis.
Price, $1750; seats 5 persons; 4 vertical, water-cooled cylinders; jump spark ignition; planetary transmission; 4 speeds; weight, 2100 pounds.

Moline, 20-22 h. p.; Moline Automobile Co., East Moline, Ill.
Price, $1750; seats 5 persons; 4 vertical cylinders; jump spark ignition; sliding gear transmission; 4 speeds; weight, 2000 pounds.

Rambler, 20-25 h. p.; Thomas B. Jeffery & Co., Kenosha, Wis.
Price, $1750; seats 5 persons; 4 vertical, water-cooled cylinders; jump spark ignition; sliding gear transmission; 4 speeds; weight, 2250 pounds.

Knox, 14-16 h. p. surrey; Knox Automobile Co., Springfield, Mass.
Price, $1750; seats 2 or 4 persons; 2 horizontal, air-cooled cylinders; jump spark ignition; planetary transmission; 3 speeds; weight, 1950 pounds.

Orient, 16 h. p.; Waltham Mfg. Co., Waltham, Mass.
Price, $1750; seats 5 persons; 4 parallel, air-cooled cylinders; jump spark ignition; sliding gear transmission; 4 speeds; weight, 1450 pounds.

Orient, 16 h. p; Waltham, Mfg. Co., Waltham, Mass.
Price, $1750; seats 4 persons; 4 air-cooled cylinders; jump spark ignition; sliding gear transmission; 4 speeds; weight, 1350 pounds.

Franklin, 14 h. p.; H. H. Franklin Mfg. Co., Syracuse, N. Y.
Price, $1800; seats 5 persons; 4 vertical, air-cooled cylinders; jump spark ignition; sliding gear transmission; 4 speeds; weight, 1300 pounds.

Reo, 16 h. p. coupe or depot wagon; Reo Motor Car Co., Lansing, Mich.
Price, $1800; seats 4 persons; 2 horizontal-opposed, water-cooled cylinders; jump spark ignition; planetary transmission; 3 speeds; weight, 1800 pounds.

Corbin, 24 h. p.; The Corbin Motor Vehicle Corporation, New Britain, Conn.
Price, $1800; seats 2 persons; 4 air-cooled cylinders; jump spark ignition; clash gear transmission; 4 speeds; weight, 1800 pounds.

The WALKER Runabout

1906

Dolson, 28-30 h. p.; Dolson Automobile Co., Charlotte, Mich.
Price, $1800; seats 5 persons; 4 vertical, water-cooled cylinders; jump spark ignition; sliding gear transmission; 4 speeds; weight, 2000 pounds.

Mitchell, 24-30 h.p.; Mitchell Motor Car Co., Racine Junction, Wis.
Price, $1800; seats 5 persons; 4 vertical, water-cooled cylinders; jump spark ignition; sliding gear transmission; 4 speeds; weight, 1800 pounds.

Northern, 20 h.p.; Northern Mfg. Co., Detroit, Mich.
Price, $1800; seats 5 persons; 2 double-opposed, water-cooled cylinders; jump spark ignition; planetary transmission; 3 speeds; weight, 2100 pounds.

Pungs-Finch, 22 h.p.; Pungs-Finch Auto and Gas Engine Co., Detroit, Mich.
Price, $1850; seats 5 persons; 4 vertical, water-cooled cylinders; jump spark ignition; sliding gear transmission; 4 speeds; weight, 1850 pounds.

Knox, 14-16 h.p.; Knox Automobile Co., Springfield, Mass.
Price, $1900; seats 5 persons; 2 horizontal, air-cooled cylinders; jump spark ignition; planetary transmission; 3 speeds; weight, 2000 pounds.

Queen, 28 h.p.; C. H. Blomstrom Motor Co., Detroit, Mich.
Price, $2000; seats 5 persons; 4 vertical, water-cooled cylinders; jump spark ignition; sliding gear transmission; 4 speeds; weight, 2,000 pounds.

Logan, 30 h.p.; Logan Construction Co., Chillicothe, O.
Price, $2000; seats 5 persons; 2 opposed, water-cooled cylinders; jump spark ignition; sliding gear transmission; 3 speeds; weight, 2155 pounds.

York, 24-28 h. p.; York Automobile Co., York, Pa.
Price, $2000; seats 5 persons; 4 vertical, water-cooled cylinders; jump spark ignition; sliding gear transmission; 4 speeds; weight, 1975 pounds.

Corbin, 24 h.p.; Corbin Motor Vehicle Corp., New Britain, Conn.
Price, $2000; seats 5 persons; 4 air-cooled cylinders; jump spark ignition; clash gear transmission; 4 speeds; weight, 1800 pounds.

Lambert, 34 h. p.; Buckeye Mfg. Co., Anderson, Ind.
Price, $2000; seats 5 persons; 4 vertical, water-cooled cylinders; jump spark ignition; friction drive transmission; weight, 2000 pounds.

Orient, 20 h. p.; Waltham Mfg. Co., Waltham, Mass.
Price, $2000; seats 5 persons; 4 air-cooled cylinders; jump spark ignition; sliding gear transmission; 4 speeds; weight, 1700 pounds.

Zent, 35 h. p.; The Zent Automobile Co., Bellefontaine, O.
Price, $2000; seats 5 persons; 4 vertical, longitudinal, air-cooled cylinders; jump spark ignition; individual cone clutch transmission; 3 speeds; weight, 1900 pounds.

Crawford; Crawford Automobile Co., Hagerstown, Md.
Price, $2000; seats 5 persons; 4 vertical, water-cooled cylinders; jump spark ignition; sliding gear transmission; 4 speeds; weight, 2100 pounds.

Duquesne, 16-21 h. p.; Duquesne Construction Co., Jamestown, N. Y.
Price, $2000; seats 5 persons; 4 vertical, air-cooled cylinders; jump spark ignition; planetary transmission; 4 speeds; weight, 1750 pounds.

Berkshire, 16 h, p.; Berkshire Automobile Co., Pittsfield, Mass.
Price, $2000; 4 water-cooled cylinders; jump spark ignition; sliding gear transmission; 4 speeds; weight, 1800 pounds.

Pungs-Finch, 28-32 h. p.; Pungs-Finch Auto and Gas Engine Co., Detroit, Mich.
Price, $2200; seats 5 persons; 4 vertical, water-cooled cylinders; jump spark ignition; sliding gear transmission; weight, 1900 pounds.

St. Louis, 30-35 h. p.; St. Louis Motor Car Co., Peoria, Ill.
Price, $2200; seats 5 persons; 4 water-cooled cylinders; jump spark ignition; sliding gear transmission; 4 speeds; weight, 2170 pounds.

Oldsmobile, 26-28 h. p.; Olds Motor Works, Lansing, Mich.
Price, $2250; seats 5 persons; 4 vertical, water-cooled cylinders; jump spark ignition; sliding gear transmission; 4 speeds; weight, 2000 pounds.

Premier, 20-24 h. p.; Premier Motor Mfg. Co., Indianapolis, Ind.
Price, $2250; seats 5 persons; 4 vertical, air-cooled cylinders; jump spark ignition; sliding gear transmission; 4 speeds; weight, 1900 pounds.

Haynes, 30-35 h. p.; Haynes Automobile Co., Kokomo, Ind.
Price, $2250; seats 5 persons; 4 vertical, water-cooled cylinders; jump spark ignition; sliding gear transmission; 4 speeds; weight, 2250 pounds.

Stoddard-Dayton, 30-35 h. p.; Dayton Motor Car Co., Dayton, O.
Price, $2250; seats 5 persons; 4 vertical, water-cooled cylinders; jump spark ignition; sliding gear transmission; 4 speeds; weight, 2100 pounds.

Orient, 20 h. p.; Waltham Mfg. Co., Waltham, Mass.
Price, $2250; seats 5 persons; 4 air-cooled cylinders; jump spark ignition; sliding gear transmission; 4 speeds; weight, 1800 pounds.

St. Louis; St. Louis Motor Car Co., Peoria, Ill.
Price, $2500; seats 5 persons; 4 water-cooled cylinders; jump spark ignition; sliding gear transmission; 4 speeds; weight, 2200 pounds.

Cadillac, 30 h. p.; Cadillac Motor Car Co., Detroit, Mich.
Price, $2400; seats 5 persons; 4 vertical, water-cooled cylinders; jump spark ignition; planetary transmission; 4 speeds; weight, 2300 pounds.

Harrison, 35-40 h. p.; Harrison Wagon Co., Grand Rapids, Mich.
Seats 5 persons; 4 vertical, water-cooled cylinders; jump spark ignition; sliding gear transmission; 4 speeds.

Stevens-Duryea, 20 h. p.; J. Stevens Arms and Tool Co., Chicopee Falls, Mass.
Price, $2500; seats 5 persons; 4 vertical, water-cooled cylinders; jump spark ignition; sliding gear transmission; 4 speeds; weight, 1800 pounds.

Moline, 30-35 h. p.; Moline Automobile Co., East Moline, Ill.
Price, $2500; seats 5 persons; 4 vertical, water-cooled cylinders; jump spark ignition; sliding gear transmission; 4 speeds; weight, 2100 pounds.

Winton, 30 h. p.; The Winton Motor Carriage Co., Cleveland, O.
Price, $2500; seats 5 persons; 4 vertical, water-cooled cylinders; jump spark ignition; individual clutch transmission; 3 speeds.

Iroquois, 25-30 h. p.; Iroquois Motor Car Co., Seneca Falls, N. Y.
Price, $2500; seats 5 persons; 4 vertical, water-cooled cylinders; jump spark ignition; sliding transmission; 4 speeds; weight, 2400 pounds.

Ford, 40 h. p.; Ford Motor Co., Detroit, Mich.
Price, $2500; seats 5 persons; 6 vertical, water-cooled cylinders; magneto ignition; planetary transmission; 2 speeds; weight, 2000 pounds.

Marion, 24-28 h. p.; The Marion Motor Car Co., Indianapolis, Ind.
Price, $2500; seats 5 persons; 4 air-cooled cylinders; jump spark ignition; sliding gear transmission; 4 speeds; weight, 2100 pounds.

Marmon, 20-24 h. p.; Nordyke & Marmon Co., Indianapolis, Ind,
Price, $2500; seats 4 persons; 4 air-cooled cylinders; jump spark ignition; planetary transmission; 3 speeds; weight, 2150 pounds.

Jackson, 40-45 h. p.; Jackson Automobile Co., Jackson, Mich.
Price, $2500; seats 5 persons; 4 vertical, water-cooled cylinders; jump spark ignition; sliding gear transmission; 4 speeds; weight, 2400 pounds.

York, 30-35 h. p.; York Automobile Co., York, Pa.
Price, $2500; seats 5 persons; 4 vertical, water-cooled cylinders; jump spark ignition; sliding gear transmission; 4 speeds; weight, 2350 pounds.

Grout (gasoline), 35 h. p.; Grout Brothers Automobile Co., Orange, Mass.
Price, $2500; seats 5 persons; 4 water-cooled cylinders; sliding gear transmission; 4 speeds; weight, 2200 pounds.

Wayne, 35 h. p.; Wayne Automobile Co., Detroit, Mich.
Price, $2500; seats 5 persons; 4 water-cooled cylinders; jump spark ignition; sliding gear transmission; 4 speeds; weight, 2100 pounds.

S T A N L E Y   S T E A M   C A R

THE FASTEST CAR IN THE WORLD

(Rate of 127.66 Miles an Hour)

This car, at Ormond, Fla., Jan. 21 to 28, 1906, established the following World's Records:

WORLD'S RECORDS		FORMER RECORDS	
1 Kilometre	$.18\frac{2}{5}$	Darracq	$.21\frac{2}{5}$
1 Mile	$.28\frac{1}{5}$	Napier	$.34\frac{2}{5}$
1 Mile in Competition	$.31\frac{1}{5}$		$.41\frac{2}{5}$
5 Miles	$2.47\frac{1}{5}$	Napier	3.17
2 Miles (World's record for cars eligible under the rules)	$.59\frac{3}{5}$		

The 5-mile record was made in competition, with a scoring start, and was at the rate of a mile in $33\frac{2}{5}$ seconds, which is faster than any gasolene car built according to A. A. A. rules ever made for a single mile.

The power-plant in this car is exactly like that in the regular Stanley cars, except that it is larger, of about twice the power as the Touring Cars (Model F). It weighs 1,600 pounds, and has margin enough for another boiler of the same size (512 pounds) without passing the racing weight-limit of 2,204 pounds. The boiler is 30 inches in diameter and 18 inches deep. It contains 1,475 tubes, and has a total heating surface of 285 square feet. A steam pressure of 800 to 900 pounds is carried. The engine is $4\frac{1}{2}$ x $6\frac{1}{2}$, and makes 350 revolutions to the mile. The wheels are 34 inches in diameter, and make 600 revolutions to the mile. They are equipped with 3-inch G. and J. tires. The body is so designed that the largest cross-section it presents, including the wheels, is only 9 square feet.

Reo, 24 h. p.; Reo Motor Car Co., Lansing, Mich.
Price, $2500; seats 5 persons; 4 vertical, water-cooled cylinders; jump spark ignition; sliding gear transmission; 4 speeds; weight, 2000 pounds.

Upton, 24-30 h. p.; Lebanon Motor Works, Lebanon, Pa.
Price, $2500; seats 5 persons; 4 vertical, water-cooled cylinders; jump spark ignition; sliding gear transmission; 3 speeds; weight, 2400 pounds.

Apollo, 35 h. p.; Chicago Recording Scale Co., Waukegan, Ill.
Price, $2500; seats 5 persons; 4 water-cooled cylinders; jump spark ignition; sliding gear transmission; 4 speeds; weight, 2100 pounds.

Dolson, 38-40 h. p.; Dolson Automobile Co., Charlotte, Mich.
Price, $2500; seats 5 persons; 4 vertical, water-cooled cylinders; jump spark ignition; sliding gear transmission; 4 speeds; weight, 2250 pounds.

Rambler, 35-40 h. p.; Thos. B. Jeffery & Co., Kenosha, Wis.
Price, $2500; seats 5 persons; 4 vertical, water-cooled cylinders; jump spark ignition; sliding gear transmission; 4 speeds; weight, 2700 pounds.

Buick, 30-35 h. p.; Buick Motor Co., Jackson, Mich.
Price, $2500; seats 5 persons; 4 vertical, water-cooled cylinders; jump spark ignition; sliding gear transmission; 4 speeds; weight, 2000 pounds.

Elmore, 35 h. p.; Elmore Mfg. Co., Clyde, O.
Price, $2500; seats 5 persons; 4 vertical, water-cooled cylinders; roller contact coil and battery ignition; sliding gear transmission; 4 speeds.

Cadillac, 30 h. p.; Cadillac Motor Car Co., Detroit, Mich.
Price, $2500; seats 5 persons; 4 vertical, water-cooled cylinders; jump spark ignition; planetary transmission; 4 speeds; weight, 2400 pounds.

Pope-Hartford, 20-25 h.p.; Pope Mfg. Co., Hartford, Conn.
Price, $2500; seats 5 persons; 4 vertical, water-cooled cylinders; jump spark ignition; sliding gear transmission; 4 speeds; weight, 2250 pounds.

Berkshire, 25 h.p.; Berkshire Automobile Co., Pittsfield, Mass.
Price, $2500; seats 5 persons; 4 vertical, water-cooled cylinders; jump spark ignition; sliding gear transmission; 4 speeds; weight, 2300 pounds.

Buick, 30-35 h.p.; Buick Motor Co., Jackson, Mich.
Price, $2500; seats 5 persons; 4 vertical, water-cooled cylinders; jump spark ignition; sliding gear transmission; 4 speeds; weight, 2000 pounds.

The Lambert and Rolls-Royce, 1907

Below, left, is a 1907 Lambert manufactured in Anderson, Indiana. The car featured a friction-drive transmission, a type in which no gears were used but a sliding disc mounted on a jackshaft engaged a flat disc mounted at the extreme rear end of the crankshaft. By movement of the lever, the sliding disc on the jackshaft could be set at any one of many positions, thus offering different gear ratios. The closer the sliding disc was to the center of the crankshaft disc which transmitted the power, the more power was passed along to the rear wheels. As a youngster living in Berthoud, Colorado, I recalled a local farmer who purchased a Lambert car and drove it with his family to his old home in Indiana over dirt roads. This proud owner of an early Lambert claimed he had no trouble outside of replacing several of the friction discs.

A name in the car world which has always had a royal ring to it is Rolls-Royce. The 1907 "Silent Six" Rolls, pictured below, right, was a touring car which sold for $8,000, could travel at speeds up to 60 miles per hour, and boasted of 40 to 50 horsepower. Needless to say, $8,000 was an enormous amount of money to pay for an automobile, or anything else, in 1907.

1907

30-40 H. P. Silent Six Cylinder Touring Car, $8,000 Complete.

"Practically Noiseless," 1907

In 1907 Stoddard-Dayton was one of America's fine automobiles. Their copy writer was not above doing a little knocking in his claim that *some* motorcars in motion "sound like a boiler shop on a busy day as they creak, pound and groan with rheumatic regularity." The Stoddard-Dayton machine, on the other hand, kicked up no such fussy racket but moved along as smoothly as the grease and oil with which all running parts were lubricated. It so happens that this copy writer had it right; this was an excellent motorcar, one that deserved to survive but didn't. This five-passenger model had a four-cylinder motor and sold for $2,500.

A Practically Noiseless Car

SOME motor cars in motion sound like a boiler shop on a busy day. They creak, pound and groan with rheumatic regularity. Their running parts seem to be aching joints relieved only by these noisy evidences of mechanical ills and disordered make-ups.

Stoddard=Dayton

machines kick up no such fussy racket. They move along as smoothly as the grease and oil in which **all running parts** are packed. **Every pound of power** that is coming to you in **speed** and **mileage** is a **certain** Stoddard-Dayton WEARING ASSET.

In our Model-F 5-passenger touring car the **noiseless qualities** of preceding models have all been retained, and in our new Stoddard-Dayton 4-cylinder motor—cylinders cast in pairs—a **perfect** system of lubrication is maintained **independent of splash.**

The Stoddard-Dayton will equal the performance of any American-made car, at any price, as to speed, power, control and durability.

Model-F is a 30-35 H. P. high class car; transmission sliding gear, selective type, 3 speeds and reverse; 34 inch wheels; enclosed fenders; equipped with strut rods, which **take all strain** off rear springs, now hung **on** shackles at both ends.

Thoro tests prove **higher** efficiency of new motor 4⅝ x 5.
Price $2,500, including front and rear lamps. Our 1907 Auto-Book gives splendid description of all our machines. Let us send it to you—FREE.

THE DAYTON MOTOR CAR CO., DAYTON, OHIO.

Cars Built in Various Cities

In early days, automobiles were manufactured in almost any city, town, or hamlet where the builder could get together equipment to start his venture. Many pioneer car manufacturers had been manufacturers of wagons, buggies, road carts, and threshing machines. When the buggy maker saw that he was losing his market to the automobile, he often figured that his buggy customers would follow him and buy an automobile bearing his name. This did not prove to be true, however, as not a single buggy manufacturer survived in the manufacture of passenger cars, except Studebaker.

Shown on this page are two cars, the McIntyre (top, left) and the Babcock (below, middle), both produced by widely known buggy manufacturers. At bottom, left, is the Crawford car, built by a firm in Hagerstown, Maryland. This car passed out of the picture soon after this 1909 ad appeared.

Below, right, is the Sharp "Arrow," manufactured at Trenton, New Jersey. Much is made in this ad of the fact that Mr. Sharp, as an amateur driver, had great success in his first race when he set a record of 56.7 miles per hour for 188 miles in the Motor Parkway races of 1908. Automobile companies paid a great deal of attention to the results of such early races in order to place their product before the public in the best light.

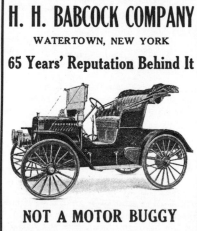

Famous Early Names

The Winton Six (below, left) was a favorite of many early American motorists. The 1910 model shown at right had many innovations. Winton pioneered self-starting with an air starter which occasionally didn't work but, generally speaking, was quite satisfactory. Many automobile historians credit the founder of this make, Alexander Winton, with the sale of the first gasoline auto in this country. In 1898, Mr. Winton built four gasoline cars and succeeded in selling one of them to a skeptical buyer.

At right, below, is the Cartercar Model T friction-drive truck built in 1910. This light truck with double chain drive, wood artillery wheels, and rubber tires was among the first successful light delivery gasoline vehicles. Throughout the years Cartercar was favorably known as manufacturer of friction-driven automobiles which gave good satisfaction and service in their time. Later, the Cartercar Company became one of the many acquisitions of General Motors, but lasted only a very short time. Over the years General Motors bought up a number of such smaller companies—Elmore, Reliance, Sheri-

dan, Scripps-Booth, Welch—which ultimately disappeared from the scene entirely.

Although the name Franklin always was best known in the passenger-car field, the firm also built a few trucks. Shown below, right, is a 1910 model with such well-known Franklin features as an air-cooled engine, full elliptic front springs, and a progressive sliding gear transmission. Notice the bulb horn and kerosene lamps. With four tires in the rear, this model undoubtedly was one of the first dual-tire-equipped vehicles. In 1910, there were 181,000 passenger cars produced; 6,000 trucks and buses were manufactured, almost twice as many as the year before.

The Nyberg Six

In 1912 the Nyberg Automobile Works of Chicago offered some classy models ranging from a two-passenger roadster with gas tank in the rear to a seven-passenger touring car.

The ad refers to a Chicago office, a "northern factory" at Anderson, Indiana, and a "southern factory" in Chattanooga. The Nyberg was one of many assembled cars which were in vogue at the time. Note the question, "Is the price we ask too low?"

Style in 1912

By 1912, the fast-developing auto industry was already well out of its infancy. 356,000 passenger cars rolled out of the factories. In a race sponsored by the Chicago Automobile Club, the famous driver Ralph De Palma drove a Mercedes 240 miles at an average speed of 68.4 miles per hour to win top honors. Elsewhere in the industry, General Motors in 1912 adopted the electric self-starter, pioneered by Cadillac, as standard equipment. In all, 356,000 cars were manufactured in 1912, of which 78,000 were Fords. A year earlier, in 1911, the whole industry had produced only 199,000 cars. By 1914 the figure was over a half million.

The sporty 1912 cars shown on this page have all long since disappeared from the scene. The Maxwell (bottom, right) was a going concern in the early twenties when it was bought by Chrysler, but the parent company ultimately stopped manufacturing this particular make.

Model 6-50—$2850.

1912 · Sampson 35

$1325 fully equipped without top

Maxwell "Messenger"

II. Early Auto Fashions

Horseless-carriage Fashions

Wearing apparel for the early female motorist came in a variety of styles. But first, and foremost, these outfits had to protect as large an area as possible from the hazards of open driving. Dust coats, or dusters, as they were commonly known, came in many designs for both men and women. The motorist shown below, right, in his complete outfit was both protected and fashionable in 1908.

In 1904 *Outing* magazine observed: "The only thing about a car which a woman does not have to teach herself with patience and skill is how to dress for it. From the first the long, graceful motor coats have appealed to women who go a-motoring. Far from being unbecoming, the rather bewildered fashions in motor chapeaux frame a pretty face enchantingly." Or so they thought in 1904.

The drawing (below, center) illustrates what the well-dressed Englishwoman wore while driving a car in 1908. The hood covers almost the entire upper portion of the head and face, but it had side windows so that Madame could quickly notice vehicles coming from either direction.

A "Windshield" Hat

Motorists in the first years of the present century were warned by doctors against "the many dangers of the open road, poisonous fumes, currents of cold air, or in the summertime, choking dust and swarms of small winged insects." A pair of good goggles always helped, but they left the upper air passages vulnerable. Until windshields and closed cars came into vogue the solution shown at left was offered to those women brave enough to venture out in all kinds of weather. This device was never popular.

In 1910 there were no tourist cabins, and movie actresses sometimes had their dressing rooms and living quarters in their cars. This happens to be a Studebaker which was converted into a rolling home. The photo below, left, was taken on a movie location in the Mojave Desert of Southern California.

For the continental touch, it would be hard to better the French demoiselle's bloomers (below, right). She is riding a motor tricycle in an automobile parade at Longchamps, near Paris, in 1905.

Smart Spring Styles Shown For Motorists.

IN MOTORING styles a more interesting display of Spring coats has never been shown, according to the leading fashion houses. Numerous smart models have been exhibited in which the detail arrangement of trimming, pockets, etc., are the distinctive features. While the fashionable shades run about alike, these coats often appear similar, but the wearer finds an extraordinary variety in their details. In the coat model at the right, one of these shown by James A. Hearn & Sons, the square pockets, pearl buttons and convertible collar all add to the smartness of the garment.

Above all things the woman who motors must needs have a suitable and comfortable hat. A fetching B. Altman & Co. model, shown here, is in a cherry colored Palm Beach straw, with facing of satin in self tone. The only trimming consists of a deep silk tassel and a band of grosgrain ribbon.

With the coming of warmer weather flowing scarf veils for automobilists are again putting in an appearance. The one illustrated here shows only one of the many fetching ways a veil may be used to good effect for both appearance and comfort on the tour.

Photos by Joel Feder, New York.

Some stunning large check fabrics are used in very distinctive topcoats, as in the model in the centre. Conspicuous among the color combinations is the simple black and white mixture. The one illustrated is a coat showing a smart belt effect and deep, novelty pockets. Black broadcloth is generously used to trim the convertible collar, cuffs and pockets.

Gold crossbar velour makes up very attractively in the smart motor coat shown on the left. The lines are quite straight, though there is ample fullness throughout the garment. Deep pockets, ornamented with novelty bone buttons, and the convertible sailor collar are especially interesting.

Woman at the Wheel

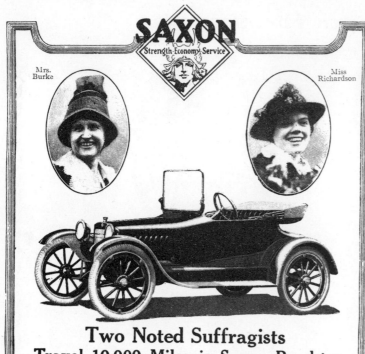

Car manufacturers were quick to broadcast valuable publicity when prominent women motorists used their automobiles. At left is a 1914 advertisement in which Saxon publicizes a nationwide tour by two women suffrage leaders, Mrs. Alice Snitzer Burke and Miss Nell Richardson. Below, right, two fashionable ladies under immense bonnets settle themselves behind the tiller of a clean, silent Baker Electric in 1905. Electrics were favored by the weaker sex because they required no cranking and there were no obnoxious exhaust fumes to contend with. Their top speed was 15 to 20 miles per hour, and most electrics would travel 20 or 25 miles on one charging of the batteries.

THOMAS FLOOD

Motoring Togs

The proper attire for early-day motorists was considered quite important, as evidenced by the illustrations on this page. Below, left, is shown an enthusiastic motorist, vintage 1921, smiling over a warm scarf made of brushed angora. The price was $10.50 and the special motoring coat of leather set the young lady back $65.

George Booss, an importer and maker of fashionable furs, offered the unique and undoubtedly expensive Russian pony motor coats in 1907, below. Mr. Booss had a Fifth Avenue address and undoubtedly catered to the ritzy crowd with his distinguished offerings. For those who felt that their drivers should also be fashion plates, Mr. Booss offered special "chauffeurs' outfits."

George Booss

Importer and Maker of

Fashionable Furs

294 Fifth Avenue   New York

Russian Pony Motor Coats

A large and varied assortment of Motor Coats and Chauffeurs' Outfits constantly on hand

Everything in High=Class Furs

Illustrated Catalogue mailed upon request

Peter Helck

Just about the only American artist who specializes in depicting old automobiles is Peter Helck of New York, pictured below, right, in his famous Locomobile "Old 16." He has painted the classic racing events of Europe and the United States and is himself a car collector. His esteem for early cars stems from their unstyled integrity, he says. "They were road vehicles, designed for land transportation . . . not yet . . . the target of the stylists who view such earthbound utilities as carpet sweepers, book ends, and refrigerators as objects for aero stylization."

Left: The artist's interpretation of the finish of the ninth Vanderbilt Cup Race (294 miles) in Santa Monica in 1912, which Ralph De Palma won in a 1908 Mercedes.

Below: In 1903 the Paris-Madrid race was stopped at Bordeaux because of too many fatalities. The winner was M. Gabriel in an 80-horsepower Mors car which averaged 65.3 miles per hour for the 342 miles, without a tire change!

Historical Auto Paintings

In 1908, the New York to Paris race—via Seattle, Japan, and Siberia—was won by Americans Montague Roberts and George Shuster in a Thomas Flyer built in Buffalo. Mr. Helck's interpretation, stars and stripes flying, is below.

. . . The first idol of the race tracks, colorful, cigar-smoking Barney Oldfield (pictured at bottom, in his Peerless "Green Dragon"), performed many spectacular feats and won many records on early racing tracks.

III. An Automotive Society

Gas Stations and Blacksmiths

It is doubtful if anyone could identify the far-sighted fellow who opened the first real gasoline filling station or service station in the United States. Certainly the two stations shown here are among the earliest. The one at the right was a drive-in emporium at the corner of Oak and Young streets in Columbus, Ohio, run by the Standard Oil Company as early as 1901. Before this time, gas had been sold house-to-house. Below, center, is a building supposed to have housed the first gasoline station in the Northwest, operated by the Wadhams Oil Company. Early gas-station attendants and blacksmiths had three kinds of horseless carriages to worry about, two of which (electric and steam) needed attention but no gas.

At right is a village blacksmith's shop of the type which many car owners visited for repairs in those days. When my father, Dr. J. B. Clymer, a small-town physician and surgeon, bought his first curved-dash Oldsmobile in 1902 it was the village blacksmiths in Berthoud, Colorado, A. G. Bimson, Andy Berglin, and the Preston brothers, who did most of our repairing. They welded springs, straightened axles, soldered radiators, and poured babbitt for new connecting rods and main engine bearings. The blacksmiths of America were the true pioneers in servicing the earliest motorcars.

Slow Beginnings

Pioneer motorists had a great deal of trouble with the law. As early as 1895 Chicago had a regulation banning the use of automobiles on the public streets. The picture below, left, shows Elwood Haynes, the Kokomo, Indiana, inventor, being stopped in one of his earliest cars by a Chicago policeman mounted on a bicycle. He, like so many others, was told to remove the car from the streets.

Among other freak early laws was one which required a motorist to stop his car and fire off a Roman candle when a horse-drawn vehicle came into view, as shown at the bottom of the page. Many cities had ordinances restricting automobiles to speeds as low as 2 or 3 miles per hour, and in some cities a car could not be driven after dark.

Around 1905 a representative in the Massachusetts Legislature, afraid of life and limb, introduced a bill requiring cars to have a bell which would ring once for each wheel revolution (below). Fortunately for all concerned, the idea found few backers. The early autoist had enough to worry about without having to contend with the wild imaginations and fears of his timid neighbors. Roads were often muddy ruts, spare parts were difficult to obtain, and supplies of water and gas were never just around the next bend in the road. There were no carefully numbered highways or precise filling-station maps, and motorists were continually losing themselves in country lanes and elsewhere.

Sportsmen

The first motorists were hardy types. Among them were many avid sportsmen. In 1905 a man named Fitch, shown behind the wheel in the top photograph, and a sportsman passenger went on a hunting excursion to the Canadian deer country in a White Steamer. Note the rugged terrain and thick brush they had to plow through.

The hunters at the bottom are driving a four-cylinder car known as "Reo the Fifth," and the company's famous slogan "You can do it with a Reo" apparently went along for the ride. Ransom E. Olds, designer of the Reo, stated in an advertisement that this Reo model, one of the most reliable cars of its time, was his "farewell car"—it marked the limit of his engineering knowledge. He could build nothing better.

Small-town Automobiliana

Farmers and residents of small towns were among the first buyers of automobiles. It was not uncommon on a summer evening or a Sunday morning to see a group of cars gathered for various forms of competition in these localities. More peaceful car fans formed auto clubs and scheduled picnics and country outings.

Such a meeting is shown in the two photos below. The pictures were taken at Liberal, Kansas, in 1908. The cars in the top photograph are, left to right: a two-cylinder Reo, a Model H Maxwell Touring Car with progressive sliding-gear transmission, a Buick, a Great Smith, another Reo, and a four-cylinder Maxwell. In the photograph below are several of the same cars, probably photographed the same day. The small car at the left, not in the other picture, is a Maxwell Model A.

In 1908 some 63,500 passenger cars were made. Left-hand steering had just begun to appear, and in all there were 175 automobile makers in business.

Faith, Hope, and Charity

This advertisement for automobile prints "to beautify your home" appeared in a 1909 issue of *Life* magazine (no connection with the present *Life*). The publishers offered special prices on photogravures "of the highest possible quality and finish." A real bargain—160 pictures for 25 cents! Thus the omnipresent auto crashed even the art world.

Do You Ever Go Home?

FAITH

HOPE

Then beautify your home with cheerful things. On receipt of twenty-five cents we will send you our little book of *LIFE'S PRINTS* containing 160 reproductions of these most artistic and pleasure-giving pictures.

With the catalogue you will also receive the supplement of 47 additional pictures.

CHARITY

These three subjects are printed together as one photo-gravure, 22 by 18 inches.
Price $2.00.

The prints described, whose prices are given, are *PHOTO-GRA-VURES* of the highest possible quality and finish. Neither care nor expense has been spared to attain the very best artistic results.

160 Pictures for 25 Cents

LIFE PUBLISHING COMPANY, *49 West 31st Street*, NEW YORK

Reserved Acceptance

The chauffeur's certificate of registration pictured below was issued in August, 1909, by the state of Ohio to one James McGrew. In addition to state certificates, many towns and cities required some official sort of permission to drive an automobile. Most states required registration of the car and certain cities and counties also required separate registration. In some cases two and even three sets of license plates were necessary.

The Denver street scene at lower left shows as many bicycles as automobiles, but by 1910, when this picture was taken, the public had accepted the automobile as a phenomenon that was here to stay. . . . Many a farmer made extra money by pulling stranded motorists out of the mud with a team of horses in the days before good highways were common. Perhaps the stalled motorist shown at bottom, right, had made a deal with the man in the wagon to pull him out of the mire.

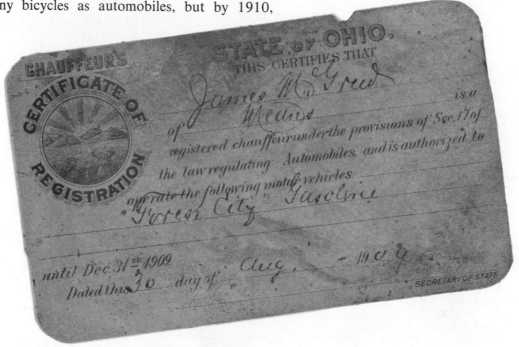

She Preferred the Horse

Nostalgia for the horse-and-buggy days asserted itself in many different ways as various and sundry people took sidelong thrusts and digs at the newfangled motorcar. This sentimental ditty by Grace Duffield Goodwin is included as a typical example.

To An Automobile
(With Apologies)
By Grace Duffield Goodwin

I have a humble longing that has never been confessed,
A longing I have striven in vain to bury in my breast;
I want to take a ride once more, when days are hot and muggy,
Behind a little jogging horse in some old shabby buggy.

I oft am hurled along the road in someone's fine machine
At such a pace I cannot tell a brown field from a green.
I want to amble on at peace, unheeding what they say,
And watch with joy an ancient horse flick ancient flies away.

I never see a landscape now that is not scudding by
In gales of wind and clouds of dust before my goggled eye;
The pensive cows are galloping, the hens are squawking past;
If anything seems peaceful I know it will not last.

I have no great ambitions and I don't desire to shine
As a heroine of accidents in the automobile line;
This my plebeian longing, without quibble or remorse—
I want that shabby buggy and I want that ancient horse!

The Omnibus Era

By 1908 the automobile was replacing horse-drawn vehicles for sightseeing purposes. Below is a Rapid two-cylinder sightseeing car with double chain drive and planetary transmission in Denver, Colorado. I recall many of these cars which were used by the Denver Omnibus and Cab Company to transport tourists who came to the "Mile-high City" for sightseeing vacations. Many localities called them "rubberneck buses." The driver usually carried a large goose-necked megaphone.

At bottom is an experimental vehicle made at Saginaw, Michigan. Even then that city was producing, in limited quantities, automobile parts used in many makes of cars. The Jackson & Church Iron Works, which made this bus, abandoned the project shortly thereafter. In the colorful tradition of auto advertising, they claimed that this bus was capable of 60 miles per hour and that no one dared "open 'er up" on the unpaved streets of 1906, even with a capable driver like Peter P. Wilkins at the wheel.

The Fifth Avenue Bus

Here are many different types of buses once operated by New York City's Fifth Avenue Coach Company. Some of them had imported chassis with special bodies manufactured specifically for traffic conditions in New York. Most early buses were equipped with solid tires and with iron spoke wheels. Many used double side chains for final transmission to the rear wheels. Few riders of today's buses appreciate the early work done by the builders of the vehicles we see here. The famous double-decker buses are fast disappearing from Fifth Avenue today.

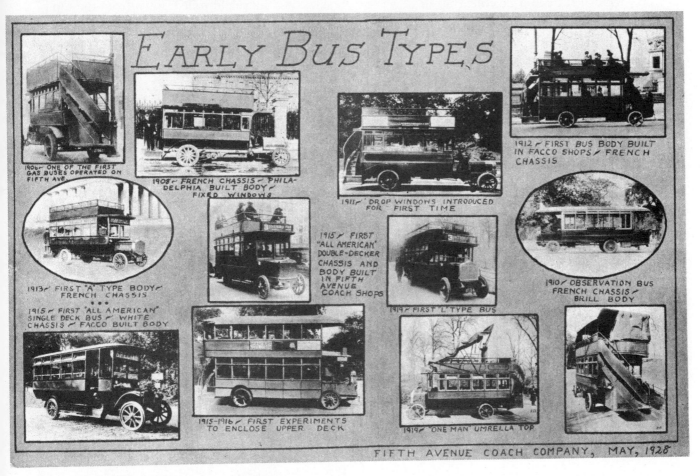

EARLY BUS TYPES

1906 — ONE OF THE FIRST GAS BUSES OPERATED ON FIFTH AVE.

1908 — FRENCH CHASSIS — PHILADELPHIA BUILT BODY — FIXED WINDOWS

1911 — DROP WINDOWS INTRODUCED FOR FIRST TIME

1912 — FIRST BUS BODY BUILT IN FACCO SHOPS — FRENCH CHASSIS

1913 — FIRST "A" TYPE BODY — FRENCH CHASSIS

1915 — FIRST "ALL AMERICAN" DOUBLE-DECKER CHASSIS AND BODY BUILT IN FIFTH AVENUE COACH SHOPS

1915 — FIRST "ALL AMERICAN" SINGLE DECK BUS — WHITE CHASSIS — FACCO BUILT BODY

1919 — FIRST "L" TYPE BUS

1910 — OBSERVATION BUS FRENCH CHASSIS — BRILL BODY

1915-1916 — FIRST EXPERIMENTS TO ENCLOSE UPPER DECK

1919 — "ONE MAN" UMBRELLA TOP

FIFTH AVENUE COACH COMPANY, MAY, 1928

At left is an early bus operated by the Watertown (Connecticut) Transportation Company. This might be classed among the first elaborate buses, yet solid tires were used with double chain drive. Passengers needed three steps to enter. This bus appeared in 1912 or 1913.

Two Early Trucks

Commercial firms were quick to replace horse-drawn trucks with powered vehicles. Below is an early Reo operated by the Coca-Cola Bottling Company in Dothan, Alabama. The final drive was by double chain. Solid tires still were in vogue when this picture was made in 1911. The cab's windshield could be rolled up or down to afford some protection for the driver. Gas for the large headlights alongside the windshield was supplied by a Prest-O-Lite tank.

Some trucks, such as the 1911 White (at bottom), had combination tire equipment. Pneu-matic tires with demountable rims were used on the front wheels, solid tires on the rear wheels. The body apparently was made by some builder of wagon bodies in the days when streamlining wasn't too important. Protection from the weather was available by rolling down side curtains. A windshield rolled down from the top of the cab, but vision through celluloid windows was somewhat limited. The driver here is Henry Kramer, today a veteran of forty-three years with the Jackson Storage and Van Company of Chicago.

The Legal Aspect

Once upon a time, motorists were confronted with a number of unusual and in some instances discriminatory laws. Cleverly placed "auto traps" were the least of the motorist's worries. Police in some areas were authorized to shoot at tires and stretch ropes, chains, or wires across the road. By 1909 the Automobile Club of America was up in arms. They raised funds to defend their arrested members, appealed cases to higher courts, and wrote angry articles. They charged that policemen were discriminating against the owners of powerful and expensive cars (who presumably could pay large fines) while the smaller cheaper cars, making greater speed or driven with less care, were allowed to pass through the speed traps unmolested. "It is impossible to avoid the feeling," the *Metropolitan Auto Guide* stated indignantly in 1909, "that the financial result often figures. . . . This is arbitrary exercise of police power, a mixture of persecution and retribution." The magazine went so far as to offer its readers maps on which were marked the exact location of auto traps and "prejudiced" constables and pointing out special areas and small towns where the local speed limit was something lower than a sluggish crawl. . . . The poem below appeared in 1904.

THE VILLAGE MOTOR-TRAP

Screened by a wayside chestnut tree,
   The village "P. C." stands,
The "cop," a crafty man is he
   With a stop watch in his hands,
And the muscles of his lower jaw
   Are set like iron bands!

He goes each morning to his lair
   And hides among the trees,
He hears the sound of motors there
   And it sets his mind at ease,
For it seems to tell of captures—and
   Promotion follows these!

Folks often call his statement lies
   And his ruse a "shady" plan.
But he *knows* his watch is accurate!
   And he stops whoe'er he can.
And he looks the motorist in the face
   For he fears not any man.

From morn till night he's timing there
   The cars that come and go,
While his stop watch ticks the seconds off
   With measured beat and slow,
Nor thinks of rest till he homeward turns,
   When the evening sun is low.

Hiding and clocking, summoning,
   Onward through life he goes.
Each night he's had his vengeance on
   Some of his "scorching" foes.
Somebody summoned, someone "done,"
   Has earned a night's repose.

Thanks, thanks to you, ye zealous "chaps"
   For the lesson you have taught,
For now we read in "thicket," "traps,"
   And, warned, we go uncaught.
For where the trees are thickest—there
   We know such deeds are wrought.

   —"Pedal and Crank," in *The Motor*, London

The Cyclecar Craze, 1910–1916

The cyclecar can perhaps be considered a first cousin of the motorcycle and bicycle. Some 125 different makes of cyclecars were manufactured in the United States, most of them appearing between the years 1910 and 1916. This was the era of the extreme lightweight automobile, and many were equipped with motorcycle tires and wheels.

Two-cylinder air-cooled engines and four-cylinder water-cooled engines were used by many of the cyclecar makers, and in some instances, belts were used for final drive instead of chains or shaft.

A 1914 cyclecar list (below) shows 38 cars with additional information on seating, horsepower, lubrication, cooling, ignition, and other items. At left is a light sporty Grant Car which in 1913 was rated at 15 horsepower and weighed 930 pounds. Perhaps the most unique cyclecar of all was the Imp, manufactured in Auburn, Indiana. It had a tandem seating arrangement and was powered by a motorcycle engine; a single long V-belt transmitted the final drive. These light cars were considered exceptionally maneuverable and the better models traveled from 40 to 50 miles or better on a gallon of gas.

Make	Seats	W. B.	Trd.	Wgt.	Cy.	Bore	Stroke	H. P.	Cooling	Lubrica-tion	Carburetor	Ignition	Trans-mission
Ajax	side by side	..	..	....	4	2.20	3.80	10	water	pump	special	......	friction
Brown	side by side	96	44	600	2	...	...	10	air	......	Schebler	Bosch	friction
Car-Nation	side by side	104	48	1050	4	3.12	3.75	..	water	pump	Car-Nation	......	selective
Car-Nation	tandem	104	48	1150	4	3.12	3.75	..	water	pump	Car-Nation	......	selective
Comet	tandem	100	36	....	2	3.50	3.67	10	air	......	Schebler	Bosch	planetary
Cornelian	side by side	100	56	450	2	2.37	2.90	..	......	......	......	......	selective
Cricket	side by side	82	46	....	2	3.25	3.60	8	air	......	......	......	selective
Davis	tandem	93	36	475	2	3.50	3.67	10	air	......	Schebler	Bosch	selective
Dayton	tandem	104	36	550	2	3.50	3.62	9-13	air	......	Schebler	Bosch	friction
Dayton	side by side	104	36	550	2	3.50	3.62	9-13	air	......	Schebler	Bosch	friction
De Cross	tandem	98	36	....	2	3.50	3.62	10-12	air	......	Schebler	Bosch	friction
Detroit	side by side	92	44	....	4	2.75	4.00	12	water	gravity	Schebler	Bosch	selective
Downing	side by side	103	56	670	2	3.50	3.67	12	water	gravity	Schebler	Bosch	selective
Downing	side by side	103	56	670	4	2.75	4.12	18	water	pump	Schebler	Bosch	selective
Dudly	staggered	96	40	500	2	...	...	10-13	air	......	Schebler	At. Kent	planetary
Duryea	side by side	102	..	....	2	3.75	3.75	19	air	......	Heitger	option	friction
Economycar	tandem	106	36	393	2	3.50	3.62	8-10	air	gravity	Schebler	Bosch	planetary
Falcon	staggered	96	36	325	2	3.37	3.90	10	air	......	Heitger	......	friction
Faultless	staggered	100.5	36	....	2	3.37	3.87	..	air	......	......	......	friction
Fenton	side by side	96	36	500	2	3.50	3.67	10	air	pump	Schebler	Bosch	friction
Imp	tandem	100	36	600	2	3.50	3.67	10-15	air	pump	Schebler	Bosch	friction
Lavigne	side by side	96	50	600	4	...	...	..	air	......	Schebler	Bosch	selective
Los Angeles	side by side	102	44	450	2	3.37	3.87	10	air	pump	......	......	friction
Los Angeles	side by side	102	44	500	4	2.50	3.50	12-15	water	pump	......	......	friction
Malcolm	tandem	100	36	560	2	...	...	10-15	air	pump	special	......	friction
Mercury	tandem	100	36	....	2	3.50	3.50	9.8	air	gravity	Schebler	Bosch	friction
Pioneer	staggered	96	44	500	2	2.87	4.00	12-15	air	pump	Schebler	Briggs	friction
Princess	side by side	86	44	725	4	2.75	3.87	12	air	pump	Holley	Bosch	planetary
Puritan	side by side	108	42	550	2	...	...	10	air	......	......	......	planetary
Rayfield	......	96	..	....	4	2.75	4.50	12	water	......	Rayfield	Bosch	selective
Rocket	tandem	100	36	650	2	3.50	3.67	10-12	air	gravity	Schebler	At. Kent	planetary
Stickney	tandem	120	40	....	4	2.75	5.00	12-15	water	......	Schebler	Bosch	friction
Trumbull	side by side	80	44	650	4	2.87	4.00	14-18	water	pump	......	At. Kent	friction
Twombly	tandem	96	38	....	2	...	...	10	air	......	......	Bosch	friction
Twombly	tandem	102	38	....	4	...	...	15	water	......	......	Bosch	selective
Victor	side by side	98	..	....	4	3.37	3.75	18	water	......	Breeze	Berling	selective
Woods	tandem	98	30	450	4	2.68	2.93	14	air	pump	......	......	planetary
Zip	side by side	92	40	600	2	3.37	3.90	10-14	air	......	Schebler	At. Kent	friction

*Any number; †front, 28x2¾ rear; ‡front, 30x3 rear.

Metz, Mercury, and Malcolm

Shown at right is the 1914 Metz Speedster, a cyclecar built on racy lines with electric lights set into the front fenders like the projecting eyes of an insect. It used a friction-drive transmission. . . . Long before Ford's Mercury car was manufactured, there was a Mercury cyclecar built in the factory shown below at 807 Scotten Avenue in Detroit. The car was belt-driven with the tandem seating arrangement. . . . One of the most advanced cyclecars with a narrow tread was the 1914 Malcolm, shown below. Note the cantilever springs and the V-belt drive. In design it had a low-slung, sleek look that today is considered quite modern. The single passenger sat directly behind the driver, not exactly an inducement to intimate conversation.

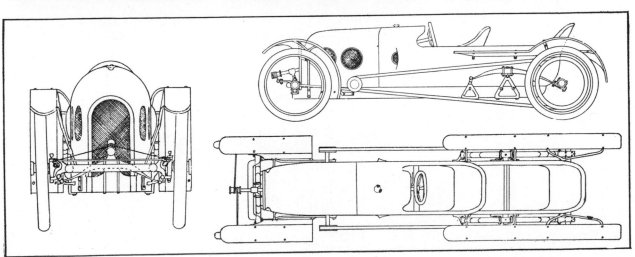

O-We-Go, Princess, and Bug

Shown at left is the diminutive 1914 Princess cyclecar with a sloping hood similar to the French Renault. The Princess ad stated that the "factory was running night and day to keep

orders up to date." The makers claimed the demand had been so tremendous that they could accept only a few more agencies.

Below is the 1914 O-We-Go cyclecar powered by an Ives two-cylinder air-cooled engine. Final drive was by belt and rear suspension was by cantilever springs. This tandem model with a very narrow tread was popular for a short time. Note the Klaxon hand-operated horn alongside the driver's seat.

The 1914 Dudly Bug, at bottom, which bears rather a resemblance to a praying mantis, had twin headlights mounted quite high on the radiator and a gaudy top for protection from the weather. Like most other cyclecar builders, the Dudly Company advocated the V-belt drive. If a prize for the homeliest car of the year was awarded in 1914, the Bug certainly must have run off with top honors.

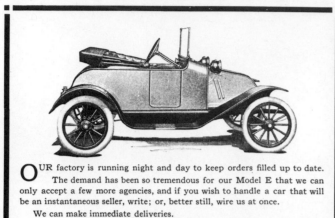

Our factory is running night and day to keep orders filled up to date. The demand has been so tremendous for our Model E that we can only accept a few more agencies, and if you wish to handle a car that will be an instantaneous seller, write; or, better still, wire us at once.

We can make immediate deliveries.

PRINCESS MOTOR CAR COMPANY
348 CLAY AVENUE, DETROIT

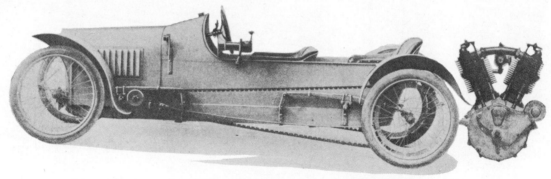

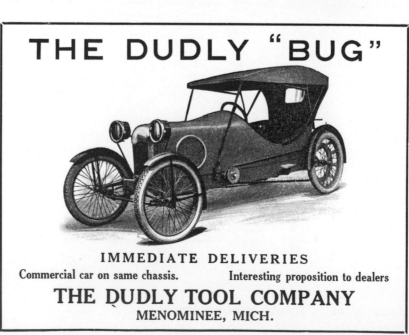

THE DUDLY "BUG"

IMMEDIATE DELIVERIES

Commercial car on same chassis.   Interesting proposition to dealers

THE DUDLY TOOL COMPANY
MENOMINEE, MICH.

Car-Nation

One of the best of the cyclecars was the four-cylinder Car-Nation, which was built by the makers of the well-known Keeton car. The Car-Nation cost $495, f.o.b. Detroit, and traveled 25–30 miles per gallon. The Keeton adapted "the best of foreign practice" to U. S. needs.

Passenger "Six-48" KEETON

$3250 Completely Equipped

KEETON
THE TWO CARS THAT WILL INCREASE YOUR SALES
CAR=NATION

The volume of your sales largely depends upon the attraction value of the cars you handle. Some cars feature power, some economy, some quietness, others speed, appearance, price, etc., but in no other car will you find these qualities blended in such harmonious proportions as in the new "Six-48" Keeton.

A limited number of these "distinctive" cars will be produced for the coming season and dealers will find it greatly to their advantage to get in touch with us at once.

KEETON SPECIFICATIONS

Electric starting. Full electric light equipment. Six cylinders cast en bloc, large valves. Small bore, long stroke. All moving parts completely enclosed. Exceptionally powerful and flexible. Radiator at rear of motor in proper and protected position. Centrifugal pump and fly wheel fan insure ample cooling. Four speeds forward in transmission. Direct on 3rd—geared up on 4th. Left hand drive—right hand control. Wire wheels—with extra detachable wire wheel. Long 136-inch wheel base—long springs, special alloy spring steel, nearly flat under load. Chrome Vanadian Gears and Shafts on imported annular bearings. Pressure gasoline feed. Very roomy and comfortable bodies. Best of foreign practice adapted to American road and touring conditions. Very complete and detailed equipment.

PRICES F. O. B. DETROIT

2 Passenger Roadster completely equipped	$3250.00
7 Passenger Touring Car completely equipped	$3250.00

A full line of open and closed bodies. Interesting literature sent on request.

$495.00 $495.00

CAR-NATION
"The Car for the American Public"

More Than a Cyclecar

The Car-Nation has all the features hitherto only found on large expensive cars, yet it is light, snappy, economical (25-30 miles to the gallon) and the price is within the reach of the great majority of buyers.

The Car-Nation is made of standard parts, every one of which has been time tried and proven by use in bigger cars costing $1000 and over. Just think of what this means in *every day service* to an owner.

Read the specifications and go over them part by part with any car you can think of. The 4-cylinder block motor with 3 speed forward and reverse, selective type transmission and multiple disk clutch as a unit power plant—wire wheels. Left hand drive center control—V shaped radiator with a sloping hood and cowl—in fact every part is a "feature" in many larger cars.

DEALERS—We *are now producing* these cars and the territory is going fast. You can make a very advantageous connection by closing your territory for this line. Write or wire now.

See Our Exhibits at New York and Chicago Shows

2 Passenger "CAR-NATION" Plowing the Mud

CAR-NATION SPECIFICATIONS

Unit Power Plant—Motor—4-cyl. en bloc 3¾x 3¾ "L" head—large valves and bearings. Very quiet and powerful. Ignition—Magneto —Fixed Spark. Lubrication—Constant Level Splash—Plunger Pump. Carburetor—Approved Type—very economical. Cooling—Thermo Syphon. V shaped radiator—adjustable belt driven fan. Clutch—Multiple steel disk type running in oil. Transmission—Selective type 3 speeds forward and reverse. One lever control. Drive—Bevel gear through concentric torque tube with one universal joint. Rear Axle—Semi Floating Type, Hyatt Roller Bearings. Brakes—Emergency, Internal Exp. on 10" drum on rear wheels. Service external contracting on transmission shaft. Wheels—Detachable wire—30x3" clincher rims and smooth tread tires. Control—L. H. drive center control. Wheel base 104". Tread 48". Standard equipment—Horn—Head Lamps and Tail Lamp with set of tools.

PRICES

Model A—2 Passenger Roadster- - - -	$495.00
Model B—2 Passenger Tandem Type - -	$510.00
Model C—4 Passenger Touring Car - -	$520.00
Extra Equipment—Top, $25.00 ; Windshield, $10.00	

Manufactured by KEETON MOTOR CO., Detroit, U. S. A.

Steam Cars Were Popular

Ingenious Yankee inventors tinkered with steam vehicles for a good part of the nineteenth century. As early as 1805, one Oliver Evans drove his "amphibious steam dredge" through the streets of Philadelphia. In some cities one found steam-powered fire engines, huge panting beasts that made a frightening racket going to and from conflagrations. In the 1860s, Frank Curtis built a horseless fire engine for the Newburyport (Massachusetts) fire fighters. . . . In 1878 the Wisconsin legislature, seeking to stimulate the development of steam carriages, offered a large money prize to the winner of a steam-wagon

race. Only two cars were entered, one weighing some 7 tons. The 7-ton Goliath ended up in a ditch, but the other steam wagon managed to complete the race. After taking a good look at the results, the Wisconsin legislators cut the prize in half because they considered the winning vehicle neither cheap nor practical.

In England, in 1833, almost seventy years before the gasoline car appeared on the scene, Dr. Church's steam omnibus (below, left) was puffing back and forth between Birmingham and London. It ran on solid tires, advertised "22 inside and 22 outside seats," and made 14 miles per hour until English law set 3 miles per hour as the limit. Later it was decreed that every steam-driven vehicle must be preceded by a man with a red flag.

Shown at bottom are two views of a 1903 White Steamer manufactured by the White Sewing Machine Company of Cleveland. The White was one of the most popular steamers. The condenser, which looks like a radiator, was used to turn the steam, after it had been used, back into water. The front seat was divided, and rear seat passengers entered through a back door. Note the kerosene headlamps and the horn fastened to the steering wheel.

Three Stanley Steamers

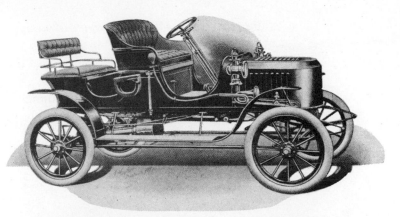

Twin inventors and developers of the steamer in America were F. O. and F. E. Stanley, identical twins from Newton, Massachusetts. They cut their beards alike, dressed alike, and their intimates were of the opinion that they even thought alike. F. O. and his wife climbed Mt. Washington in one of their early cars; others won many races and hill-climbing contests. Ultimately, in a complicated financial deal, the Stanleys sold the rights to their car to the Locomobile Company. Yet the Stanley name remained in the field even after F. E.'s death, in an auto accident, in 1917, and F. O.'s death some 22 years later.

At right (top) is a Stanley Model Ex Runabout with an open rear seat, vintage 1908. The second photo is one of Col. W. F. "Buffalo Bill" Cody at the wheel of his Model O White Steamer. The picture was taken in 1913. Third from top, right, is another Stanley, the Model 78, 20-horsepower, two-passenger roadster. The price in 1913 was $1,640. At bottom, right, is a Stanley Mountain Wagon, also made in 1913. This vehicle hauled twelve passengers, had a 30-horsepower engine, and cost $2,300. Below, left, is one of the very early electric models, the Loco-Surrey No. 5, which sold in 1903 for $1,200.

White Steamers

The White Company offered a variety of body styles in their unique steam cars. At the left is a 1905 White Bus that covered a distance of 6.51 miles in eight daily round trips between Osaka and Sakai, Japan. At the lower right is the 1905 "Double Phaeton" model with a rear entrance tonneau. The top was detachable but not collapsible. Many early-day White owners removed the top in the summertime and replaced it for winter use.

At lower left is the ritzy 1905 Model E White Landaulette. This car was built for the carriage trade. The passengers entered from the rear and were more or less sheltered, but the driver had no protection against the weather.

The late Dowager Queen Mary of England rode in a stately White Steamer in 1907 when she was Princess of Wales (circular photo below).

Truman's Stafford

Sometimes information about a particular make of automobile, produced years ago and for only a short time, proves difficult to obtain. Such was the case with the Stafford, once manufactured in Kansas City. Ultimately I learned that former President Harry S. Truman's first car was a Stafford and I wrote him a letter of inquiry. His gracious response, full of valuable information about the car, is reproduced at right. Later I spent an interesting half hour with Mr. Truman in his office in Kansas City. A man with a remarkable memory, he recalled that his Stafford had a four-cylinder engine with overhead valves and was driven by an overhead camshaft and roller tappets (a racing-engine design). He remembered that his car was No. 314 and that the last Stafford, No. 315, was made for Mr. Stafford's own personal use.

HARRY S. TRUMAN
FEDERAL RESERVE BANK BUILDING
KANSAS CITY 6, MISSOURI

February 9, 1953

Dear Mr. Clymer:

I appreciated most highly your enclosures of the early automobiles and tractors and the other booklets which you enclosed with your inquiry regarding the Stafford cars.

Staffords were first manufactured at Topeka, Kansas. Then Terry Stafford moved the factory to Kansas City. I think the last cars he made were in 1914 and he made the last one for himself, probably in 1915. I am not sure whether there are any of the cars in existence now or not.

Mine was a 1913 Model and was a five-passenger open car with straps attached to the top that buckled to the front part of the frame, although it was usually driven as an open car.

I had it remodeled into a hot sport roadster and took it to Camp Doniphan with me in 1917, where it was used by Battery "F" as a kind of transportation truck for ice and whatever else was necessary to be hauled around the Battery. I sold it to a Sergeant at Fort Sill in March 1918 just before I left for overseas.

I think Mrs. Stafford is still alive. If she is, I'll try to get her address for you and you can get in touch with her. There may be one of the cars in a garage somewhere.

It was an excellent car and would take an awful beating. You can be sure of that if one lasted me as long as three years, which that one did.

Sincerely yours,

Harry Truman

Mr. Floyd Clymer
Publisher
1268 South Alvarado Street
Los Angeles 6, California

The rare 1913 Stafford (at left) was restored by Engineer Gil Stafford of Rhode Island (no relation to Terry Stafford, the original builder). Mr. Stafford verified Mr. Truman's description of the car and further stated that the combustion chambers were of hemispherical design, which is clear evidence that this 1913 car had advanced engineering features. This five-pasenger touring model had a water-cooled engine, a three-speed sliding gear with reverse, and an emergency brake which operated on the clutch pedal. It sold for $2,250.

After the turn of the century, lives of most of our Presidents were closely connected with the automobile. At top left is the 1901 electric ambulance which bore the wounded McKinley on his last ride. At left center is President Taft, first President to have an official fleet at his disposal; at bottom left, Harding, first to drive his own car. Directly below, Theodore Roosevelt greets a crowd, and at bottom, Woodrow Wilson riding through the streets of Boston in a 1914 Cadillac.

At right: That thrifty New Englander Calvin Coolidge bought one of the White House cars after leaving office. . . . Herbert Hoover, below, took over the Presidency in 1928 when the nation had over twenty million cars. Nearly four million cars were produced in that year alone. . . . Franklin Delano Roosevelt (middle, right), though crippled by infantile paralysis, enjoyed driving his own specially equipped Plymouth. . . . Harry S. Truman (lower left) knew more about cars than perhaps any other President. Recently he purchased a Chrysler. . . . Lower right: President Dwight D. Eisenhower in a 1914 Rauch and Lang Electric owned by his mother-in-law, Mrs. Doud, of Denver. The photograph was taken during the 1952 campaign.

The Humorous Side

METHOD IN HIS SOLICITUDE.

The chauffeur was speeding the car along at a great rate. And He and She were nestled coyly in the back seat. After

a long silence he said:

"Are you quite comfortable, dear?"

"Yes, love."

"The cushions are cozy and soft?"

"Yes, darling."

"You don't feel any jolts?"

"No, sweetest one."

"And there is no draft on your back?"

"No, my ownest own."

"Then change seats with me."—Princeton Tiger.

BETTER BUY A FLIVVER.

Chug-Chug! br-r! br-r-r! Honk! Honk! Gillgillug—gilligillug.

The pedestrian paused at the intersection of two streets. He looked about. A motor car was rushing at him from one direction, a motorcycle from another, a steam truck was coming from behind and a taxicab was speedily approaching.

Zip-zip! Zing-glug!

He looked up and saw directly above him an airship in rapid descent.

There was but one chance for the poor man. He was standing upon a manhole cover. Quickly seizing it, he lifted the lid and jumped into the hole just in time to be run over by an underground train. —Los Angeles Times.

ALWAYS THE SAME FINISH.

"Yes," said the prospective buyer, "I always judge a motor car by its engine.

"But don't you pay any attention to its finish," asked the salesman, who had been making selling points of his car's upholstering and trimmings.

"Never! My cars always have the same finish—a brick wall or a ditch."

REAR-END COLLISION.

"I hear that lightning struck Speeder's big new automobile."

"Well, Speeder claims it was his automobile that struck the lightning."

ANOTHER RECORD BROKEN.

Powell & Justus, contractors at Punxsutawney, Pa., bought a motor truck at 10 o'clock in the morning, received it at 11 o'clock, paid the premium on an accident insurance policy at 12 o'clock, started the truck for Indiana at 12:30 o'clock and got a telephone message at 2 o'clock from the driver saying that in trying to avoid a collision with another machine he had crashed into a street car and the new truck was a complete wreck.

DANGEROUS BEASTS.

The teacher had been telling her class about the rhinoceros family. "Now name some things," she said, "that are very dangerous to get near to, and that have horns."

"Automobiles!" promptly answered Johnny.

WELL!! WELL!!

He—My clutch is awful weak.

She—So I've noticed.—Cornell Widow

VERSATILITY WORTH WHILE.

The recent marriage of Senorita Rose Chargood, daughter of a Brazilian millionaire, and Joseph Andrews Brooks of Brooklyn, N. Y., a former captain in the American Aviation Corps, was the culmination of a romance which began a few weeks previous on a Long Island automobile road.

Senorita Chargood, after waiting six hours for her chauffeur to adjust her automobile, which had broken down in the road, was helped out of her predicament by Mr. Brooks. He is a versatile linguist and spoke to the senorita in her native tongue, telling her how easily the trouble could be adjusted, and proceeded to fix her car, which he had in running order in a few minutes.

HOW THEY HANDLE AUTO TRAFFIC IN JAPAN.

A Japanese officer of the Kasuga, which came 11,000 miles to take part in the celebration at this harbor, gave me this list of the auto traffic rules of Japan, his translation being, as you can see, a rather free one:

In narrow place of road corner and bridge speed slowly.

When you pass the corner and the bridge ring the horn.

When you meet the cow or the horse speed slowly and take the care to ring the horn.

When you cross the railway, wait until the other cars pass through.

When a passenger of the foot hove in sight, tootle the horn trumpet at him melodiously at first. Then if he still obstacles your presence, tootle him with vigor and express by word of the mouth by warning "Hi!"

When anything the matter with your car you go to police station and tell him.

When two cars are driving in the same road, if there is another car behind yours or ahead of yours, you must keep 60 yards away. He must do the same. If you go ahead of him, ring horn and pass by him.—The Stroller in Portland, Me., Evening Express-Advertiser.

WHY DID THEY LEAVE THE CAR?

An Illinois man advertises in his local paper as follows: "I will give $200 reward for the arrest and conviction of the party or parties who broke into my garage and robbed my 1920 Ford touring car of top, curtains, wheels, cushions, carpets, floor boards, engine hood, radiator cap and tools."

SURE TO GET HIM.

"You're under arrest," exclaimed the officer, as he stopped the automobile.

"What for?" inquired Mr. Chuggins.

"I haven't made up my mind yet. I'll

just look over your lights, an' your license, an' your numbers, an so forth. I know I can get you for something.' "—Ex.

French Dos-à-dos

At the turn of the century the French "dos-à-dos" (right) was extremely popular. That's French for "back to back"—the rear seat was for passengers who preferred to see where they had been rather than where they were going. Many early American automobiles used the dos-à-dos seat. When I was a youngster, with my brother and sister, I rode in a dos-à-dos facing backward in my father's 1902 curved-dash Oldsmobile.

The "animated fence post" (middle, right) is one of the early electric cars apparently designed for stately gentlemen with tall top hats who liked to enter without bending over. What the old electrics sacrificed in speed, they made up in dignity, silent performance, and cleanliness.

Below, right, is one of the earliest automobiles to be seen on the streets of Los Angeles. Directly behind the driver was a seat for two passengers facing the front. A dos-à-dos seat for two passengers faced backward. This car was apparently an experimental model, as the make is unidentified.

The 1901 Knox Gasoline Runabout three-wheeler shown directly below was a forerunner of the famous Waterless Knox. This $750 car could travel 180 miles on 6 gallons of gasoline, seated two, and was manufactured in Springfield, Massachusetts.

LET'S TAKE A RIDE ON THE JITNEY BUS

Billy Bender was a spender, threw away his dough,
He worked a mill for twelve a week, but easy come
    and easy go,
To a movie he would take his girl each Wedn'sday
    night,
But Sunday was the one day he'd spend money left and
    right,
He'd get his weekly pay, to his girlie he would say:

Chorus
Let's take a ride on the jitney bus, the jitney bus, the
    jitney bus,
We'll let the neighbors see what a good sport I can be;
We'll make love, dear, back in the rear,
Where the chauffeur can't see us,
I'm not fickle,
Zip! goes the nickel, on the jitney bus.

One night Billy called on Tilly, 'twas a night in June,
He soon won her hand, and then they planned how
    they would spend their honeymoon,
She said, "Let us take a wedding trip across the sea!"
But Billy said, "You're silly, dear, no ocean trip for me,
I'll show my love for you, so I'll tell you what we'll do.

Automobiles

It is reported that more than one hundred songs pertaining to automobiles have been written. Some sixty-eight are listed here, with songwriter and date of publication. Undoubtedly the most popular ditty was "In My Merry Oldsmobile" by Gus Edwards. In 1928, when Henry Ford first produced his Model A, Walter O'Keefe wrote a colorful song entitled "Henry's Made a Lady Out of Lizzie," in nostalgic tribute to the Model T.

Love in an Automobile. 1899
By Alfred R. Dixon.
My Automobile Girl. 1900
Words and music by R. J. Morris.
My Auto Lady. 1901
By George S. Atkins.
Jes' Come Aroun' Wid an Automobile. 1902
Words by R. Melville Baker, music by Josephine Sherwood.
When Isabella Green Went Automobiling. 1902
By Harry B. Marshall.
The Girl on the Automobile. 1905
Words by Sam Lewis, music by Joe Nathan.
Old Man Shay. 1905
By Benjamin Hapgood Burt.
In My Merry Oldsmobile. 1905
Words by Vincent Bryan, music by Gus Edwards.
On an Automobile Honeymoon. 1905
Lyrics by William Jerome, music by Jean Schwartz.
Out in an Automobile. 1905
Words by Vincent Bryan, music by George Evans.
The Motor March. 1906
By George Rosey.
Take a Little Ride with Me. 1906
Words by Jack Drislane, music by Theodore Morse.
The Gay Chauffeur. 1907
By F. L. Valentine.
I Think I Oughtn't Ought To Any More. 1907
Words and music by Vincent Bryan.
When I Go Automobiling. 1907
Words and music by Wilbur Mack.
Auto Race. 1908
By Percy Wenrich.
The Benzine Buggy Man. 1908
By Clyde N. Kramer.
The Ford. 1908
By Harry H. Zickel.
I'd Rather Have a Girlie Than an Automobile. 1908
By William A. Dillon
In an Auto Car. 1908
Words by Jean Lenox, music by Harry O. Sutton.
Take Me 'Round in a Taxicab. 1908
Words by Edgar Selden, music by Melville Gideon.
The Motor Girl. 1909
Lyric by Charles J. Campbell, music by Julian Edwards.
On a Joy Ride. 1909
Lyric and music by William Kenna.
Take Me Out for a Joy Ride. 1909
Words by Ren Shields, music by Kerry Mills.
Motor King. 1910
Words by Jack Drislane, music by Henry Frantzen.
Toot Your Horn, Kid, You're in a Fog. 1910

Words by Joseph Mittenthal, music by Joseph M. Daly.
Take Me Out in a Velie Car. 1911
Words by Harold D. Bornstein and Morton H. Luce. Music by Lawrence B. O'Connor.
Bump, Bump, Bump in Your Automobile. 1912
Words by Lew Brown, music by Albert Von Tilzer
Keep Away from the Fellow Who Owns an Automobile. 1912
By Irving Berlin.
The Big Red Motor and the Little Blue Limousine. 1913
Words by Earle C. Jones, music by Richard A. Whiting.
He'd Have to Get Under—Get Out and Get Under. 1913
Words by Grant Clarke and Edgar Leslie, music by Maurice Abrahams.
The Little Ford Rambled Right Along. 1914
Words by C. R. Foster and Byron Gay, music by Byron Gay.
Ragtime Automobile. 1914
By Elmer L. Greensfelder.
That Auto Rag. 1914
Words by Hal Geer, music by Chas. M. Smith.
Gasoline Gus and His Jitney Bus. 1915
By Byron Gay and Charley Brown.
Happy Tom O'Day. 1915
Words and music by Byron Gay.
Hop a Jitney with Me. 1915
Words by Frank Corbett and Sam Shephard, music by Walter Donovan.
I Didn't Raise My Ford to Be a Jitney, 1915
Words and music by Jack Frost.
Mister Whitney's Little Jitney Bus. 1915
Lyric by A. Seymour Brown, music by Clarence Gaskill.
The Packard and the Ford. 1915
Words by Harold R. Atteridge, music by Harry Carroll.
You Can't Afford to Marry If You Can't Afford a Ford. 1915
Words and music by Jack Frost.
You Tell It, Or Jitney-Bus Joy. 1915
Words and music by Frank Hendon.
On the Old Back Seat of the Henry Ford. 1916
Words by Will A. Dillon, music by Lawrence Dillon.
Come On Papa. 1918
By Edgar Leslie and Harry Ruby.
Don't Take Advantage. 1919
Words by Howard Rogers, music by James V. Monaco.
Taxi 1919
Words by Harry D. Kerr, music by Mel B. Kaufman.

The Scandal of Little Lizzie Ford. 1921
Words by Billy Curtis, music by Harry Von Tilzer.
On a Saturday Night. 1922
Lyric by William A. Downs and John W. Bratton, music by John W. Bratton.
Cla-wence (Don't Tweat Me So Wuff). 1923
By Joe Manuel, Mack Henshaw, and Harry Jentes.
I'm Going to Park Myself in Your Arms. 1926
By Bobby Heath, Archie Fletcher, and Alex Marr.
Up and Down the Eight Mile Road. 1926
Words by Gus Kahn, music by Walter Donaldson.
(Get 'Em in a) Rumble Seat. 1927
By Jack Marshall, Carl Lampl, and Morey Davidson.
We're the Sunday Drivers. 1927
Words and music by Chas. Kenny, Irving Mills, and Sammy Fain.
Gotta Big Date with a Little Girl. 1928
Words by Harry and Charles Tobias, music by Henry H. Tobias.
Henry's Made a Lady Out of Lizzie. 1928
By Walter O'Keefe.
I Love to Bumpity Bump. 1928
By Al Sherman, Al Lewis, and Carmen Lombardo.
I'm Wild about Horns on Automobiles That Go "Ta-ta-ta-ta." 1928
By Clarence Gaskill.
Poor Lizzie. 1928
By Abner Silver and Jack Meskill.
Eddie Cantor's "Automobile Horn" Song. 1929
By Clarence Gaskill, Charles Tobias and Bennett and Carlton.
Parkin' in the Park with You. 1932
Words and music by Paul Denniker and Con Conrad.
Rollin' Home. 1934
Words by Billy Hill, music by Peter de Rose.
Riding Up the River Road. 1935
Words and music by Harry Woods.
The Trailer Song. 1936
Lyric by Joe Young, music by Fred E. Ahlert.
Our Little Home on the Highway. 1937
Words and music by Sam Coslow.
Fifteen Kisses on a Gallon of Gas. 1939
By Mack David, Arthur Terker, and Jerry Livingston.
My Beloved Is Rugged. 1942
Words and music by Seger Ellis.
The Cranky Old Yank. 1942
By Hoagy Carmichael.
My Ten Ton Baby and Me. 1942
By Meredith Wilson.

A Selden Rarity

Almost every pioneer motorist has heard of George B. Selden, who applied for and received a patent on a car he claimed to have invented in 1877. Although the Selden Patent, an important factor in the early days of the industry, was later declared invalid, the name lives on. Shown here are two photos of the little-known Selden car, invented by Arthur R. Selden, the brother of George B. Selden.

This car was described as a sport model and had many unique features. It was driven by the front wheels through a chain transmission connected with a jackshaft. Mr. Selden started work on the car in 1903, and finished in 1908. A mechanical engineer, he made all the drawings and patterns himself, as well as doing most of the machine work. The engine was a two-cylinder horizontal-opposed, four-cycle, air-cooled job, and was made by the Brennan Motor Company of Syracuse, New York. Lubrication was drip-fed from a brass tank holding 2 quarts. Ignition was the jump-spark system using dry-cell batteries. This odd one-seater had a planetary transmission with two forward speeds.

Three More Oddities

At right is some inventor's curious device for one-man transportation, which might truly be called a one-horse vehicle. The obvious question is: Why doesn't he just ride the horse? Below is a 1906 Autocar which boasted a gearshift lever, throttle, and spark controls all mounted on the steering column—positive proof that there is nothing new under the sun. In 1937 LaSalle and Pontiac "reintroduced" the steering-column gearshift lever, although it had been used by early manufacturers such as Autocar, Pierce and Great-Arrow.

The 1900 "pillbox" coupé (below, right) was one of the first convertibles. Both the windshield and the doors could be removed.

Finger-Reach Control

In this car all controlling levers are assembled at the steering post. Wheel, gear shift, clutch, throttle and spark control are all within finger reach, so that the operator need never take either hand away from the steering post. This arrangement, together with the responsiveness of the Autocar running mechanism, makes this car easier and simpler than a horse to drive. The greatest value ever offered in a light four-passenger car is

Type VIII, AUTOCAR at $1400

Horizontal two-cylinder opposed motor—no noticeable vibration. Twelve actual horsepower. Three speeds forward and a reverse. Ball bearing, shaft drive. Front and rear construction has ball bearings throughout. Gasoline tank holds 10 gallons—sufficient on good roads for 200 miles.

Engine and transmission case are accessible from above without disturbing body. Catalogue describing Type VIII, Type X Runabout, and Type XI Four Cylinder Car, with dealer's name, sent free.

THE AUTOCAR COMPANY, Ardmore, Pa.
Member Association Licensed Automobile Manufacturers.

IV. Competition and the Auto

The First Road Race

Winner of the first automobile race held in the United States (1895) was J. Frank Duryea (below, in bowler), who, with his brother Charles E., was the pioneer inventor of the Duryea car, which was originally manufactured in Springfield, Massachusetts. The average speed of the winning Duryea car was 7½ miles per hour and the route (see map below) was through Chicago to Evanston, Illinois. The event was sponsored by the Chicago *Times-Herald* and was the first actual competition held between automobiles of various makes in the United States.

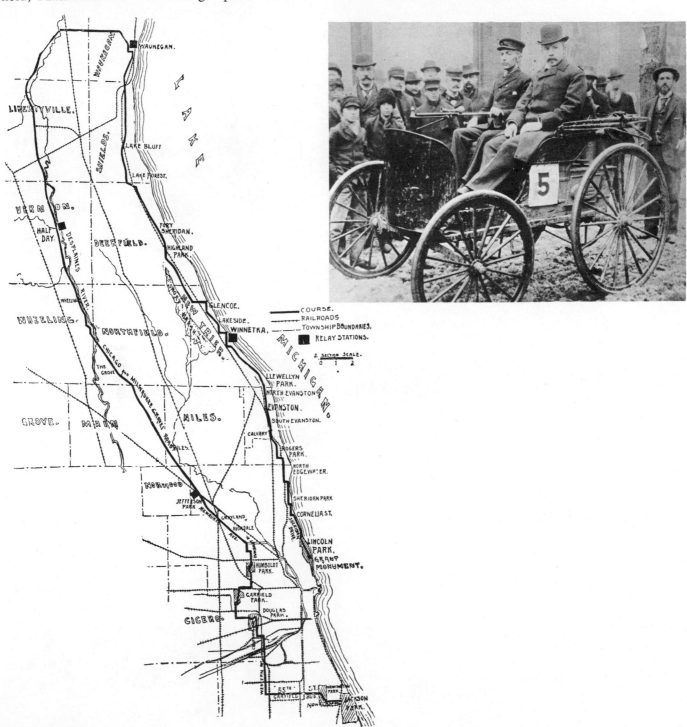

Competitive Spirit

Shown below are four White Steam Cars which won first-class certificates in the New York to Buffalo run of 1901. These were the first White Steamers to appear in open competition. Four Whites started and all four reached Rochester, where the run was canceled out of respect for the death of President McKinley.

Some of the activity at the start of the New York to Boston endurance run of 1902 is shown in the middle photograph below. The cars lined up alongside the curb for the start of the race are all White Steamers.

In the bottom photo, some of the contestants in the 1902 New York to Boston run are shown on a Boston street at the conclusion of the event.

White Steam Race Cars

Directly below are three White Steam Car winners of the Long Island endurance contest held in 1902. . . . At right is the White "Turtle" driven in 1903 at Detroit by Art Scaife. Below, right, is the 1903 White "Snail." A man named Hedges drove this car at Glenville racetrack in Cleveland. . . . At bottom, White Steamers are lined up by the Vanderbilt Mansion, New York City, before the start of the 1905 Glidden Tour to the White Mountains.

An Itinerant Blacksmith

Below is an early cartoon published by the German Automobile Club, apparently portraying a traveling blacksmith who dealt with both the horse-and-buggy and the automobile trade. This Rube Goldberg contraption could have done an enormous business in the rural districts of America when the automobile was in its infancy.

Dirt tracks were the proving grounds for automobile manufacturers in the early days. Shown below, left, is a National race car which broke the world's record for a dirt track at the Indiana State Fair Grounds at Indianapolis in 1905. In this 24-hour event, the National covered 1,094 miles, a remarkable record when you consider the date. . . . The scenic photograph below, right, shows a Stanley Steamer puffing up Mt. Washington on July 18, 1905, with Mts. Jefferson and Adams in the background. Such exciting mountain-climbing contests for automobiles helped attract tourists to the White Mountain resorts. The Hotel Mount Washington actually used this photograph in an advertisement.

Early Hot Rods

Many home-made racing cars were developed for use on half-mile and mile tracks in all regions of the United States. Shown here are a couple of early cars which might well have been termed "hot rods" of their day.

Above is a Buick Special driven by J. O. Morgan, and below, a Maxwell Special driven by H. L. Smith. Notice the extremely short wheelbases, which were considered advantageous for the short dirt tracks. Wire wheels and rubber tires of cord construction were apparently standard equipment for the "hot-rodders" before the twenties. A good proportion of these dirt-track races were run at county fairs.

Hopped-up Model T's

In race car No. 24, below, sits one of the most famous race drivers who ever competed on the dirt tracks of the Middle West. He is the late Noel Bullock, of Ord, Nebraska. In this hopped-up Model T with overhead valves, Bullock was the sensation of the dirt tracks. He also surprised the racing world when he won the famed Pikes Peak Hill Climb in 1922, driving a home-made Ford against special factory-built cars.

In the bottom photo, the unidentified driver of a Model T spared no effort in making it a snappy dirt-track competition car.

Racing Bodies for Fords

The racing body directly below is a "cut-down" 1919 Ford (Model 21 body). Its selling points were listed as follows: "The driver's seat is 7 inches forward of the seat for the passenger, thus giving more elbowroom. The seats are 13 inches lower than the regular Ford seats. The body drops 8 inches below the frame. The outside exhaust is a feature liked by some drivers of speedsters."

The middle racing body is an "Arrow" for Fords, priced at $69 (without top and windshield), and according to the copy writer, "primarily for red-blooded men who want style, dash, and snap!"

The twin racing cars at bottom, also 1919 Fords, are carrying "Roof Sixteen Overhead Valve Equipment" which allowed drivers to attain speeds of up to 100 miles per hour.

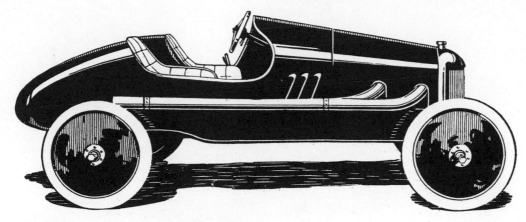

Early Days at Indianapolis

Below is Gaston Chevrolet, in mustache and goggles, in the Monroe car with which he won the 1920 Indianapolis 500-mile race. At bottom, America's World War I air ace Eddie Rickenbacker at the wheel of a Duesenberg in which he won many events on dirt and board speedways throughout the country. Years later he bought the Indianapolis Motor Speedway and operated it until after World War II. Today Rickenbacker is president of Eastern Air Lines.

Barney Oldfield's Golden Submarine

For many years Barney Oldfield's name was synonymous with automobile speed throughout the world. In the closing days of his colorful career, Oldfield competed in the unique car below, the Golden Submarine, which, because of its construction, supposedly offered added protection in case of accident. At lower left is a close-up of Barney with his proverbial cigar, sitting in the entrance of the Golden Submarine.

Lower right: Oldfield in a Marmon Model 34 Roadster after his retirement from active competition. For years after his racing days were over, he did public-relations work for various automobile factories, and also marketed a tire bearing the Oldfield name and manufactured by Firestone. This venture proved unprofitable for Oldfield and he gave up his ambitions in this field.

V. Accessories and Special Equipment

Specialties

In the days when headlights, horns, tops, windshields, speedometers, and bumpers were considered "extras," the car owner had a choice of many different brands of accessories. Shown at right is the 1905 Twentieth Century line of lamps, horns, and oil guns. A combination headlight and generator is illustrated. The generator supplied gas for the headlight by a constant dripping of water on carbide, which produced an inflammable gas. At the lower right corner of the ad is a separate generator which also supplied gas, but with this unit it was necessary to pipe the gas to the lamps through either rubber or metal tubing. This particular generator was for motorcycle use and was a smaller version of a unit adapted for automobiles.

The "Collapsible Rubber Driver" (below) is the accessory to end all accessories. So lifelike, so terrifying, absolutely guaranteed to frighten any potential car thief to death! When not in use, simply deflate, fold, and put under the seat.

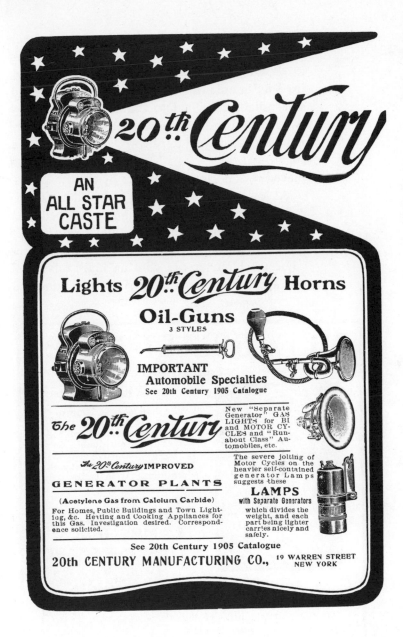

Patent-leather License Plates

License plates once consisted of a patent-leather pad to which were attached letters and numbers of bronze or aluminum similar to the ones now used for numbering buildings. The leather pad was usually attached to the car's rear axle by two leather straps. At lower left is an ad featuring Dietz kerosene lamps with fancy names—the Regal and the Orient. Kerosene lamps were replaced by gas lamps and later by electric lamps.

At lower right is an early Fisk Rubber Company ad featuring a mechanically fastened tire. The first automobiles were fitted with either solid tires or single-tube pneumatic tires. Later came the clincher tire with an inner tube, and still later, the demountable rim which consisted

of a ring that could be removed to slip the tire off the wheel easily. In 1911 the Rambler offered what was called a "fifth wheel," a forerunner of the spare tire. Spare wheels soon became standard equipment for the motorist.

Hill Holder, 1906

Below is an ingenious device used on the 1906 Thomas Flyer. Both rear wheels were fitted with powerful ratchets and pawls which were controlled from the seat. The brakes could be thrown instantly into action, thus "positively" holding the car on the steepest of hills if for any reason the motor stopped. The advantage of the Thomas Flyer system was that if the brake were released on a hill the car would remain motionless, whereas on other cars when the brake was released the car would start rolling backward.

At upper right is an advertisement for the Riley Auto Robe. Before closed cars became popular, the motorist had a knotty problem keeping warm, so numerous types of robes were offered for his comfort. Some even had pockets to insert electric heating devices.

The THOMAS BACK STOP SAFETY DEVICE

One of the minor excellencies of the **THOMAS**—the Thomas Back Stop Safety Device—is in itself so vital and so important as to be deserving of special and serious consideration.

50 H. P. $3,500

There have been safety devices put forward that are not safe; that in themselves contain elements of risk and peril. In the **Thomas** *both* rear wheels are fitted with powerful rachets and pawls which are controlled from the seat and can be instantly thrown into action. They will positively hold the car if for any reason the motor is stopped on a hill side.

It may be asked : will not the brake do the same thing? The **Thomas** has four powerful brakes, with unusual width of braking surface. But like all others they must be released when power is applied. There's where the danger lies. But the pawl need not be disengaged. It does not interfere with the car's forward motion, but will check any backing instantly.

Get the 1906 Thomas Catalogue and learn more about this invaluable feature and the other exclusive excellencies which have earned for the Thomas the title of " the most thoroughly standardized car in the world."

THE THOMAS MOTOR CO., 1201 Niagara Street, Buffalo, N. Y.
Members Association Licensed Automobile Manufacturers.

"No Tools but the Hands"

The Goodyear Tire and Rubber Company (below) optimistically claimed that 60 seconds was all the time needed in 1907 to "detach and re-attach" a tire. We've apparently been retrogressing since 1907. . . . The early car owner was an avid picnicker and liked to go on camping expeditions. The De Luxe Campstool (shown below in use, closed and open) was one of many similar contraptions which either confused or made the motorist happy. Few of these special campstools survived, and they are now just a memory to auto pioneers. . . . It's probably stretching things to include the Noiseless Vacuum Toothpick (right) in a book on automobiles, but since it was "a boon to well-bred people" (*i.e.*, all auto fanciers), here it is.

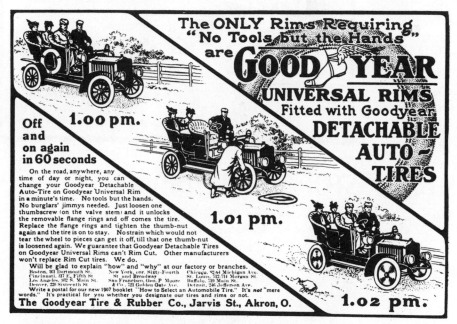

The ONLY Rims Requiring "No Tools but the Hands" are GOODYEAR UNIVERSAL RIMS Fitted with Goodyear DETACHABLE AUTO-TIRES

1.00 pm.

Off and on again in 60 seconds

On the road, anywhere, any time of day or night, you can change your Goodyear Detachable Auto-Tire on Goodyear Universal Rim in a minute's time. No tools but the hands. No burglars' jimmys needed. Just loosen one thumbscrew (on the valve stem) and it unlocks the removable flange rings and off comes the tire. Replace the flange rings and tighten the thumb-nut again and the tire is on to stay. No strain which would not tear the wheel to pieces can get it off, till that one thumb-nut is loosened again. We guarantee that Goodyear Detachable Tires on Goodyear Universal Rims can't Rim Cut. Other manufacturers won't replace Rim Cut tires. We do.

Will be glad to explain "how" and "why" at our factory or branches.

Boston, 351 Dartmouth St.   New York, cor. Sixty-Fourth   Chicago, 82-84 Michigan Ave.
Cincinnati, 327 E. Fifth St.   St. and Broadway   St. Louis, 712-714 Morgan St.
Los Angeles, 932 S. Main St.   San Francisco, Geo. P. Moore   Buffalo, 719 Main St.
Denver, 231 Sixteenth St   & Co., 721 Golden Gate Ave.   Detroit, 256 Jefferson Ave.

Write a postal for our new 1907 booklet "How to Select an Automobile Tire." It's *not* "mere words." It's practical for you whether you designate our tires and rims or not.

The Goodyear Tire & Rubber Co., Jarvis St., Akron, O.

1.01 pm.

1.02 pm.

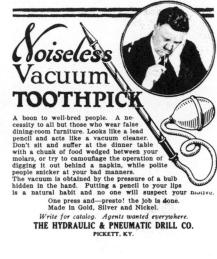

Noiseless Vacuum TOOTHPICK

A boon to well-bred people. A necessity to all but those who wear false dining-room furniture. Looks like a lead pencil and acts like a vacuum cleaner. Don't sit and suffer at the dinner table with a chunk of food wedged between your molars, or try to camouflage the operation of digging it out behind a napkin, while polite people snicker at your bad manners.

The vacuum is obtained by the pressure of a bulb hidden in the hand. Putting a pencil to your lips is a natural habit and no one will suspect your motive.

One press and—presto! the job is done.
Made in Gold, Silver and Nickel.

Write for catalog. Agents wanted everywhere.

THE HYDRAULIC & PNEUMATIC DRILL CO.
PICKETT, KY.

DE LUXE CAMP STOOL CLOSED

Stuck in the Mud?

Before paved roads, motorists faced muddy problems in rural districts during bad weather. Even as late as 1920, devices were being designed to pull cars out of the mire. The Auto Chain Pull was unusual, but it had short existence. The kind of mud into which a tire sinks hub-deep is fortunately just a bad memory to most modern drivers.

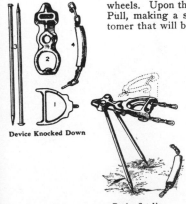

Milady's Siren

This 1906 ad for the "Long-distance Siren" also gives us an idea of what the well-dressed female autoist was wearing after the turn of the century. The immense top piece would seem about as appropriate for open motoring as it would for surf bathing, and equally difficult to keep on the head in either pursuit. Notice the very handy location of the crank operating the Long-distance Siren. In 1906 the industry produced 32,000 cars, 8,000 more than it had the year before.

Mezger's Automatic Windshield (shown below) in 1910 cost from $25 to $37.50, protected driver and passenger from cold wind in winter, and always worked—according to the claims in the ad. Many such early accessories were aimed at the "weaker sex" and its supposed inability to withstand wind, rain, cold, dirt, and the other rugged aspects of auto life. Today auto manufacturers and publicists take little notice of the differences between the sexes. Men value comfort and convenience as highly as their wives; the chest-beating outdoor type of male is out of fashion.

WARNING!

1906 THE Long Distance Siren

A Perfect Warning Signal
Clears the Way
Gives You the Road
Prevents Accidents

EVERY DRIVER of a car has experienced the uselessness of the ordinary methods for securing the right-of-way.

HOW MANY ACCIDENTS could be avoided by a proper warning signal?

HOW MUCH ADDITIONAL PLEASURE one could enjoy if sure that the road was clear?

HOW OFTEN do you slow down because you fear the driver of the vehicle ahead has not heard that **insignificant "toot"** of the bulb horn you use?

HOW OFTEN accidents occur because you thought he did hear you?

HOW about the expense?

EQUIP YOUR CAR RIGHT

The Long Distance Siren

Beautifully finished in polished brass and aluminum. All wearing parts hardened and mounted on ball bearings. A quarter turn of the handle produces a volume of sound sufficient in every case to secure the right-of-way. The sound may be soft or loud, just as wished for. Any person can attach the Siren to the car in a few minutes.

STERK MANUFACTURING COMPANY
69-71 Wells Street, Chicago, Ill.

WRITE FOR OUR ILLUSTRATED BOOKLET

MEZGER Automatic WINDSHIELD

No Dust	No Goggles
No Wind	No Rattle
No Delay	No Repairs

The window of your car—up or down in a jiffy—solid comfort whatever season you ride. Keeps off the cold wind in winter and shields you from discomfort in summer. Always ready, always works—no set-screws to tinker with—nothing to get out of order.

Made in three Types, at your dealers'—Spring Type, Spring Type with Friction Attachment, Friction Type.

Up or Down with One Hand without stopping the car.

Prices $25 to $37.50, according to Type and Size. We fill mail orders only when you mention your dealer's name, so that we can adjust the matter through him.

Send for Booklet

C A MEZGER DEPT UNITED MANUFACTURERS Broadway and 76th Street New York

Those Smug People in Ads

For several years the Kelly-Springfield Tire Company advertised widely and effectively in all types of publications throughout the United States. These amusing advertisements had many readers in their day and became the best-known and most entertaining of any series of tire ads ever to appear. For years the tire business, constantly in a state of flux, was plagued by patent difficulties and lawsuits. Eventually the Kelly-Springfield Company, which held some pneumatic-tire patents, was absorbed by the Goodyear Company.

"You don't believe in signs, do you, Cuthbert?"

"We've been pretty lucky, haven't we, Jack?   We've never had tire trouble yet."
"That hasn't been luck, dear; it's been judgment.   I've always stuck to Kelly-Springfields."

The Clymer Windshield Spotlight

In the twenties most motorists felt that a spotlight was a necessity. In 1921 I manufactured the Clymer Windshield Spotlight, which was a radical departure from conventional designs. The light was mounted through the windshield glass and operated on a ball-and-socket joint. Control was by a pistol-grip handle within easy reach of the driver. The hole in the windshield was drilled by a special glass cutter using a slotted brass tube, driven at high speed by a small electric drill. This cutter, with the aid of Carborundum and water, actually ground the hole in the glass, rather than cutting it. The Clymer Spotlight became a popular automobile accessory and for several years was sold throughout the world.

Balloon Tires and the Detachable Top

High-pressure pneumatic tires gave way to balloons in 1923 and 1924. At lower left is a Goodrich Balloon Cord ad in which the copy writer used high-pressure tactics in extolling their new low-pressure tire. This Goodrich ad compared riding on balloon cords to riding in a parlor car and likened the old high-pressure tires to riding in a day coach.

About the same time the Rex Manufacturing Company, among others, offered a detachable top to replace the folding top. It is not known where the idea originated, but in view of the fact that most of these special attachments were referred to as "California tops," it is probable that the idea originated on the West Coast. The combination summer-winter top is shown here on a 1924 Hupmobile. In winter the car would be a hard-top closed model; in summer, with little effort, the sides and top could be removed to convert into an open model.

VI. Cars for Expensive Tastes

Luxury in 1908

It's hard to remember, but at one time a Cadillac (one cylinder) sold for a third of the price of certain Ford models. Early in the history of the automobile, however, Henry Ford decided that the industry's best bet was the inexpensive car produced for a mass market, and for the most part, history has proved him correct. Most of the truly de luxe cars on the following pages, which once sold for four and five thousand dollars, are no longer manufactured. But they were magnificent machines while they lasted—as is the Cadillac today.

One of the most famous body makers in pioneer days was Brewster and Company in New York City. Shown below, left, is a Brewster body on a 1908 Renault Landaulet. . . . Illustrated

below, right, is a Carter Car (no connection with the Cartercar manufactured in Detroit). It was a luxury car with twin engines which could be operated either together or independently. Notice the two starting cranks at the front.

1908

Pope-Hartford, Berkshire, and Cudell, 1909

The Pope-Hartford, a splendid high-priced automobile, was manufactured in Hartford, Connecticut. The 1909 model pictured directly below was called the "Model R Pony Tonneau." At lower left is a 1907 Berkshire. Its slogan was "Made and Tested in the Berkshire Hills." Many claims were made for this four-cylinder, 35-horsepower car, among them that it could negotiate all grades and conditions found in the Berkshire Mountains. That made it a "good car anywhere," in the words of the Berkshire ad.

Lower right: Many European cars were imported in 1907, and the fashionable Cudell was one. This firm advertised a Royal Standard body or King of Belgium body. The car had a four-speed transmission with direct drive, and despite the crank in front, it could be started from the seat. Two-cylinder and four-cylinder models were available. A one-year guarantee and free tuition for drivers were added inducements.

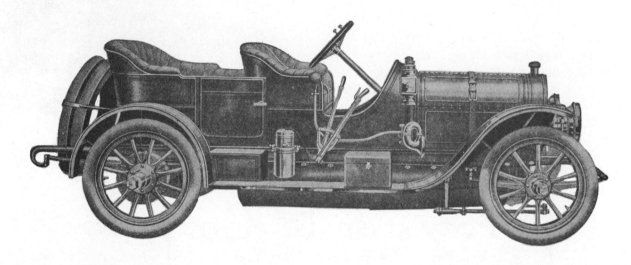

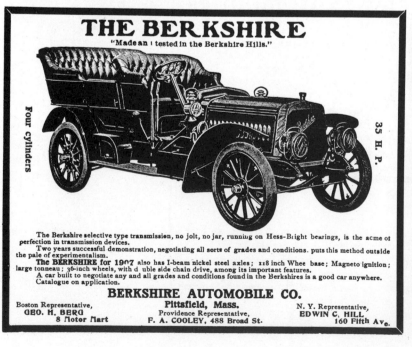

A "Vestibuled" Limousine, 1912

The luxurious 1912 Thomas Six-Forty sold for $5,150. It was manufactured by the E. R. Thomas Motor Company of Buffalo, builders of the celebrated Thomas Flyer that won the New York to Paris race in 1908. Thomas built his first cars in Buffalo in 1899, with $80,000 capital, and for many years his name was highly regarded all through the automotive industry.

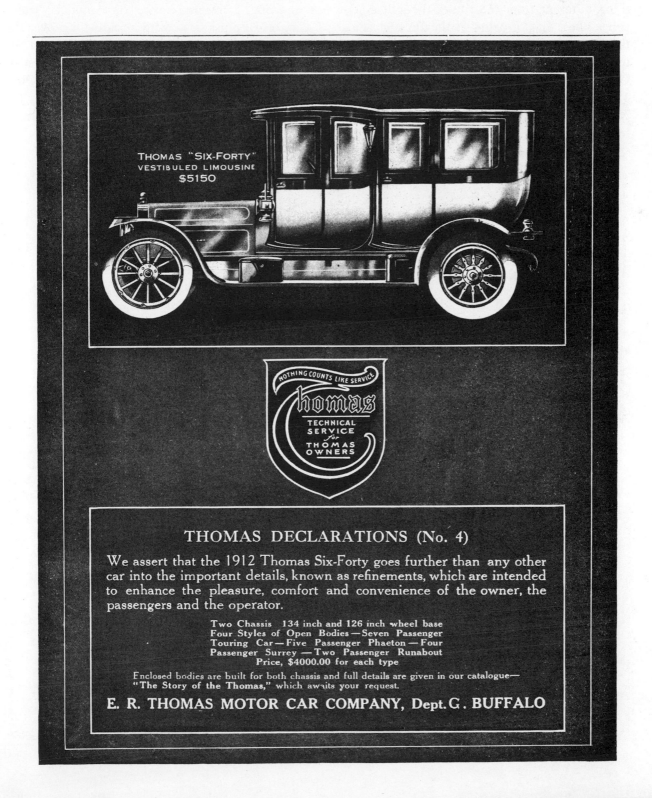

THOMAS "SIX-FORTY"
VESTIBULED LIMOUSINE
$5150

NOTHING COUNTS LIKE SERVICE

Thomas

TECHNICAL
SERVICE
for
THOMAS
OWNERS

THOMAS DECLARATIONS (No. 4)

We assert that the 1912 Thomas Six-Forty goes further than any other car into the important details, known as refinements, which are intended to enhance the pleasure, comfort and convenience of the owner, the passengers and the operator.

Two Chassis 134 inch and 126 inch wheel base
Four Styles of Open Bodies — Seven Passenger
Touring Car — Five Passenger Phaeton — Four
Passenger Surrey — Two Passenger Runabout
Price, $4000.00 for each type

Enclosed bodies are built for both chassis and full details are given in our catalogue—
"The Story of the Thomas," which awaits your request.

E. R. THOMAS MOTOR CAR COMPANY, Dept. G. BUFFALO

Pic Pic and Dagmar, 1920

In one era foreign automobiles with special custom-built bodies and sometimes with special engines were brought into the United States and sold to the well-heeled few who wanted something different from the run-of-the-mill American makes. Shown below is the Pic Pic, which the makers proudly announced was manufactured in French factories that built the famous Gnome Rotary and Rhone aviation engines. In 1920 the Pic Pic featured a pointed radiator, wire wheels with clincher tires, and a spare tire mounted on the side. As was common with most chauffeur-driven cars, the passengers could use a speaking tube (shown at the driver's right) to communicate with the chauffeur.

At bottom is a cartoon by Erwin L. Hess showing a Dagmar, one of America's early makes of plush cars, with a folding top over the rear seat and, again, no protection offered the driver. The envious young chap with the shattered romance is driving a Briggs and Stratton Flyer with a Smith Motor Wheel mounted on the rear which propelled the little vehicle at about 20 miles per hour.

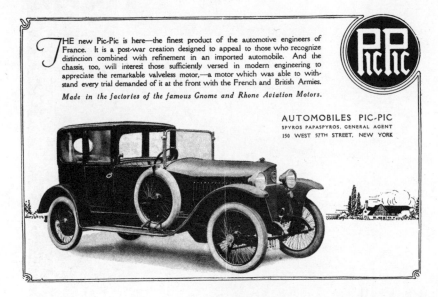

THE new Pic-Pic is here—the finest product of the automotive engineers of France. It is a post-war creation designed to appeal to those who recognize distinction combined with refinement in an imported automobile. And the chassis, too, will interest those sufficiently versed in modern engineering to appreciate the remarkable valveless motor,—a motor which was able to withstand every trial demanded of it at the front with the French and British Armies.

Made in the factories of the famous Gnome and Rhone Aviation Motors.

AUTOMOBILES PIC-PIC
SPYROS PAPASPYROS, GENERAL AGENT
150 WEST 57TH STREET, NEW YORK

THE GOOD OLD DAYS
by Erwin L. Hess

WE STILL INSIST THAT OUR SPORTY LITTLE FLYER SHATTERED ALL RECORDS FOR POPULARITY, BUT WE DO ADMIT THAT THE BIG, BRASSY JOBS DID SHATTERING, TOO .... THEY SHATTERED YOUNG ROMANCES.

YOU SAY THE FELLA WHO OWNS THAT CAR IS IN THE HOUSE RIGHT NOW WITH YOUR SISTER AN' HE'S GONNA GIVE HER A RIDE IN IT?

THAT'S WHAT I SAID!

The Sturdy Haynes, 1921

Elwood Haynes was an early automobile manufacturer from Kokomo, Indiana. In fact he claimed, mistakenly, to have fathered the first American gasoline car to run successfully, on July 4, 1894. For years he was a partner of the Apperson brothers and manufactured Haynes-Apperson cars. On his own he later manufactured an excellent high-grade car for several years. Shown at top, right, is a 1921 model which Haynes advertised as "the sensation of the new year" in that it was smaller and lighter than previous Haynes cars. Notice the square type of coupé body which was popular in the twenties with many prominent makers. A divided windshield that could be adjusted so the top portion could be set at any angle was another feature; a third was the side ventilators which were manually controlled from inside the car. No bumpers appear on this Haynes, as in 1921 they were not yet standard equipment.

The second drawing below is of the Haynes seven-passenger Suburban. The disc wheels were optional equipment on all models at extra charge. Again we have the square body effect and the side ventilators. A man with a silk top hat had no trouble in entering sedans built in the twenties. How times have changed!

In the photograph below is the 1920 Special Locomobile Touring Car. According to the Locomobile advertising "this large and luxurious vehicle was designed to combine the seven-passenger capacity of the usual large touring car with the long graceful lines of the smaller *type sportif*."

Threshing Machines and Autos

The J. I. Case Threshing Machine Company of Racine, Wisconsin, once was in the automobile business and manufactured excellent cars. Below, top, is the Case Jay-Eye-See Roadster, which was truly a sporty model in 1922. Like many well-established firms in the early days of the motorcar industry, the Case Company felt it could cash in on its reputation as builders of fine steam traction engines and threshers. . . . Shown below, center, is the Jay-Eye-See five-passenger sedan, also a 1922 model. . . . For some time the J. I. Case Company also had a powerful racing car called the Jay-Eye-See, shown below, a racing monster in which Louis Disbrow, Joe Jagersburger, and Sig Haugdahl established many records.

Custom-built Bodies

Movie stars and V.I.P.'s in the Gay Twenties invested in custom cars. The three below were built by the Don Lee Company, the top two on Cadillac chassis, the bottom one, Packard.

DESIGNED AND CUSTOM-BUILT BY DON LEE

Touring Car for Miss Anne May, *on Cadillac Chassis.*

Town Car for Mr. Jack Pickford, *on Cadillac Chassis.*

Touring Car for Mr. Henry Lehrman, *on Packard Chassis.*

Plush Interiors

Fine craftsmanship predominated in Don Lee custom-built interiors. The outdoor seating arrangement (bottom) looks sportier than it does safe.

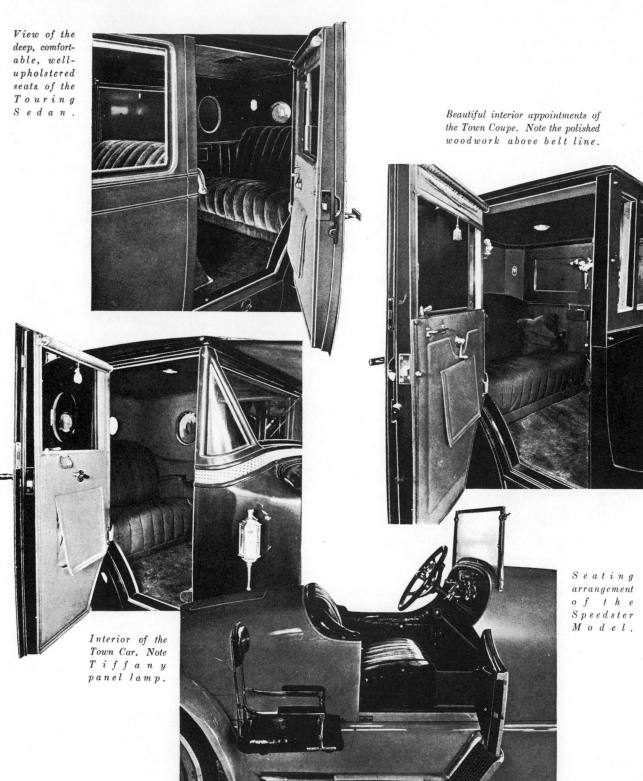

View of the deep, comfortable, well-upholstered seats of the Touring Sedan.

Beautiful interior appointments of the Town Coupe. Note the polished woodwork above belt line.

Interior of the Town Car. Note Tiffany panel lamp.

Seating arrangement of the Speedster Model.

A Price Comparison, 1907–1926

The well-to-do in 1907 could buy an open three-seater Craig Toledo (below)—"a car of manifest and extraordinary excellence"—for $4,000. Fourteen years later, in 1921, he could buy a solid, enclosed Ferris Sedan (right), one of eighty-one makes once built in Cleveland, for $4,875. The seven-passenger Pierce-Arrow four-door Coach (below, right) sold for $3,350 in that boom year 1926 to "those families who employ a chauffeur but at times who want to drive without a chauffeur."

$4,000 F. O. B. Factory

¶ A car of such manifest and extraordinary excellence—a chassis so costly—that it will upset all your previous notions of which is really the finest car made in America. We urge upon you nothing but this: ride in the Craig-Toledo. We will abide by the results.

THE CRAIG-TOLEDO MOTOR CO., Toledo, Ohio

*7-passenger, 4-door Coach
—body by Pierce-Arrow*

Pierce-Arrow's *complete line* of Custom-built COACHES
brings 73 per cent increase

WIDER and still wider grows the circle of Pierce-Arrow ownership—and with it the dealer's opportunity. The introduction of the *Series 80* line instantly increased our market eighteen times. Now with the first complete line of custom-built coaches we again add thousands of new buyers to our potential market, namely:

"Seven-passenger" families who have been waiting for a large capacity coach. ¶ *Those who want a coach but prefer the four-door arrangement.* ¶ *Those families who employ a chauffeur but at times want to drive without the chauffeur.*

Already the effects of this complete coach line have been felt. Sales of *Series 80* cars increased 73 per cent during **March, 1926**, as compared with March, 1925.

There are now splendid dealer opportunities in several desirable buying centers.

The Pierce-Arrow Finance Corporation offers dealers a complete financing and insurance service on both new and used vehicles at low rates. Write or wire us for further details.

THE PIERCE-ARROW MOTOR CAR COMPANY
Buffalo, N. Y.

PIERCE-ARROW

Custom-built Coach Bodies	
5-passenger, 2-door Coach	$3150
5-passenger, 4-door Coach	$3250
7-passenger, 4-door Coach	$3350
7-passenger, 4-door Limousine-coach	$3450

*Bodies by Pierce-Arrow; Standard SERIES 80 chassis;
soft finish, wool upholstery; six unusual color choices*

Custom-built DeLuxe Bodies			
4-passenger Coupe	$3695	5-passenger Sedan	$3895
7-passenger *Enclosed Drive Limousine*			$4045
7-passenger Sedan	$3995	Runabout	$2895
4-passenger Touring	$3095	7-passenger Touring	$2895

All prices are quoted f. o. b. Buffalo, N. Y., Reduced tax extra

Custom Roadsters

Late in the twenties, some of the special bodies so much in vogue were truly beautiful creations, such as the ones illustrated here. At left is a 1929 Cadillac V-8 Roadster with wire wheels and drum-style headlights. Notice the spare tire carried in each front fender well, and the large searchlight mounted on the left running board. The windshield could be folded to a horizontal position. The radiator shutters are automically controlled by thermostat, and a Boyce Moto-meter is mounted on top of the radiator cap, so that the driver would know the water temperature at all times. . . . Directly below, is a 1929 Rolls-Royce with a custom body. Drum headlights, white-wall tires, and wire wheels of Rudge-Whitworth make are used. . . . At left below is a 1930 Packard Eight Series 745. As in other roadsters of the period, wire wheels are used and a metal cover encases the spare tire. Adjustable windshield wings, twin spotlights, parking lights on fenders, and a rear-view mirror clamped to the spare tire are unique features. Notice the imitation grillwork in front of the radiator and the radiator-cap ornament.

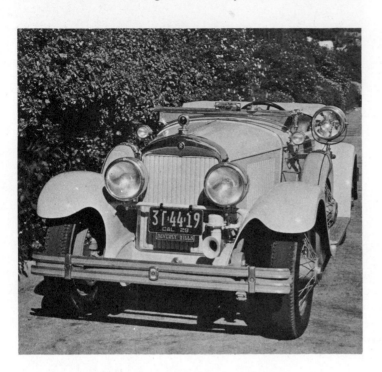

Auburn Quality, 1932

By 1932 the Auburn Automobile Company was in its last stages of automobile production. Through the years Auburn had manufactured better-than-average automobiles. Even as early as 1908 the Auburn featured a two-cylinder horizontally opposed engine. The make was well known by owners and highly respected within the automobile industry.

During Auburn's last years the car was manufactured by E. L. Cord, who also controlled Duesenberg and the front-wheel-drive Cord. It is unfortunate that these three lines of distinctive—and, in many respects, superior—makes of cars passed from the American automotive picture. Cord was considered one of the great sales geniuses of the business.

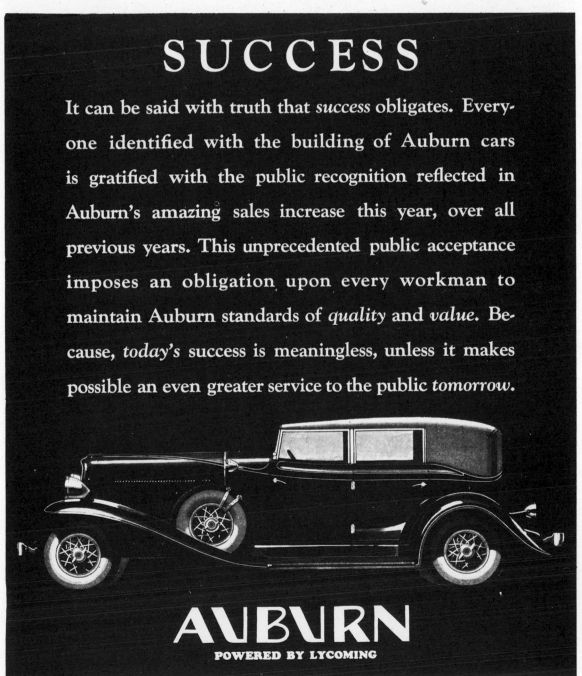

SUCCESS

It can be said with truth that *success* obligates. Everyone identified with the building of Auburn cars is gratified with the public recognition reflected in Auburn's amazing sales increase this year, over all previous years. This unprecedented public acceptance imposes an obligation upon every workman to maintain Auburn standards of *quality* and *value*. Because, *today's* success is meaningless, unless it makes possible an even greater service to the public *tomorrow*.

AVBVRN
POWERED BY LYCOMING

VII. The Restoration Movement

Antique-car Collections

In recent years antique-automobile enthusiasts have taken up the hobby of restoring old cars. Many of these restored cars are in better condition today than when they were delivered to the first purchaser years ago. Shown below is a group of cars lined up on the lawn of the Atlantic City (New Jersey) Country Club. At bottom is a partial list of some forty-one museums and collectors of automobiliana all over the United States.

LIST OF ANTIQUE CAR MUSEUMS AND COLLECTIONS IN THE UNITED STATES *

Larz Anderson Collection, Veteran Motor Car Club of America, Brookline, Mass.

Antique Auto Club, Downington, Pa.

Automobile Old Timers, New York, N. Y.

Automotive Museum, Inc., New Britain, Conn.

Belcourt Museum, Newport, R. I.

Fred and Richard Bissell Collection, Dubuque, Iowa

T. Walton Chapman Collection, Strattanville, Pa.

Henry Ford Museum, Dearborn, Mich.

Genesee Valley Antique Automobile Club, Rochester, N. Y.

Goyette Museum of Americana, Peterboro, N. H.

William Gregor Museum, Flint, Mich.

Horn's Cars of Yesterday, North Tamiami Trail, Sarasota, Fla.

Horseless Carriage Museum, Centerport, N. Y.

Kelsey's Antique Car Museum, Albert Lea, Minn.

Long Island Automotive Museum, Southampton, N. Y.

Los Angeles County Museum, Los Angeles, Calif.

Lyons Collection, Wakefield, Mass.

Marshall Museum, Yorklyn, Del.

The James Melton "Autorama, Hypoluxo, Fla.

James Melton Museum, Norwalk, Conn.

Pierce A. Miller, Rte. 1, Box 1856, Modesto, Cal.

Murchio's Motor Car Museum, Greenwood Lake, N. Y.

Museum of Antique Autos, Princeton, Mass.

Museum of Motor Memories, Indianapolis, Ind.

Museum of Science and Industry, Jackson Park, Chicago, Ill.

Old Timers Auto Museum, Scranton, Pa.

Powers Automobile Museum, Southington, Conn.

Preservation Society of Newport County, Newport, R. I.

St. Petersburg Horseless Carriage Museum, St. Petersburg, Fla.

Shirley Antique Car Museum, Shirley, Mass.

Smithsonian Institution, Washington, D. C.

Stevens Institute, Hoboken, N. J.

Swigart Museum, Inc., Huntingdon, Pa.

Taylor Museum, Canton, Conn.

Bob Thierolf's Collection, Beloit, Kans.

Thompson Products Auto Album and Aviation Museum, Cleveland, Ohio

Upstate Auto Museum, Bridgewater, N. Y.

Joseph B. Van Sciver Collection, Philadelphia, Pa.

Alton H. Walker Collection, Monterey, Calif.

George Waterman Collection, Providence, R. I.

Wolfpen Auto Museum, Southboro, Mass.

* There are many more individual collections in the United States not listed because their owners do not offer them for inspection by the public.

First Race Rerun

In 1946, under the sponsorship of the Museum of Science and Industry in Chicago, a race was run from Chicago to Evanston, Illinois, and return, to commemorate the route of the first automobile race held in America more than fifty years earlier in 1895. A large and varied group of cars participated in the rerunning of this historic event. Maj. Lennox R. Lohr directed this frigid but historic re-creation, and Miss Priscilla Lohr led the parade down Chicago's Michigan Avenue in a Sears Auto Buggy.

At left, the author (left) and co-driver John Eaton in a 1904 curved-dash Oldsmobile. The car in back is a single-cylinder Cadillac. Below is Reuben Delaunty in a Schacht friction-drive high-wheeler No. 19, followed by Clymer and Eaton. At bottom, left, the "race" rolls along past modern Chicago skyscrapers.

Chicago Was Amused

Various famous early makes participated in the rerunning of the Chicago-Evanston race. Below, left, is a portion of the crowd which gathered around the antique cars as they stopped at Evanston for lunch. Below, right, sixteen-year-old Priscilla Lohr leans out and waves from a Sears Auto Buggy, which gave an excellent performance. The Sears was powered by a two-cylinder, air-cooled engine mounted under the body. High wheels with solid rubber tires were used. Below: We had police protection from modern traffic.

The Glidden Tour Revival, 1946

The most famous endurance runs ever held in the United States were the Glidden Tours, which were sanctioned by the A.A.A. as reliability road tests until 1913 and did a great deal in the way of publicizing our automotive industry. The first tour was held in 1904, after which they were held annually for nine years.

Shown below is a reenactment of a Glidden Tour in August, 1946: the finish of the tour at the Harvey Firestone homestead at Columbiana, Ohio; at bottom, right, some tourists en route from Cleveland to Columbiana, winding through scenic Ohio; at lower left, Les Taylor tunes up his 1912 Hupmobile.

Melton's Antiques

The White Stanhope was an outstanding steam car of its day. The photograph directly below shows a 1902 model, replete with driver and passenger decked out in turn-of-the-century costumes. The eagle-eyed reader will note, however, that the steamer isn't going anywhere because there is no chain in the rear sprocket. Looks nice anyhow. . . . Opera singer James Melton, an avid collector and restorer of antique autos, led the Golden Jubilee parade in his early White Steamer (below, right) through the streets of Detroit in 1946. Mr. Melton is the driver in the bowler hat. Note the dusters worn by his two passengers. The resplendent auto at bottom, with Mr. Melton again at the wheel, is a 1910 Corbin "Cannonball."

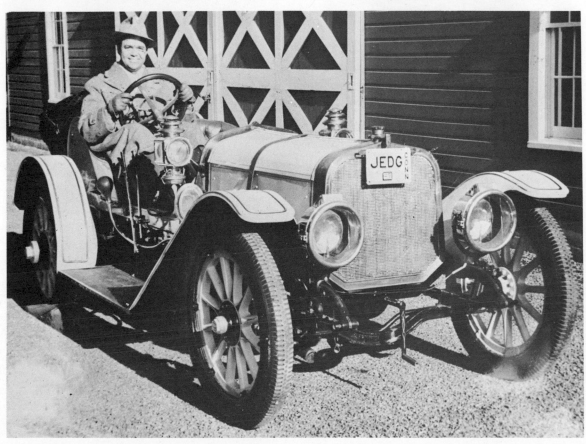

Hollywood Restores Them

Most motion-picture studios are careful to use historically accurate makes and models of cars. At left is a 1912 Ford Roadster with a "mother-in-law" seat, used in the picture "Captain Eddie." The driver is Fred MacMurray and the young lady is Lynn Bari.

Below is a 1910 Overland Roadster powered by a four-cylinder engine. This attractive two-seater had right-hand drive. Note the speedometer mounted on the right of the windshield with a cable running to the front wheel.

At bottom, a 1911 Studebaker E-M-F "30" five-passenger Touring Car. This model had the transmission just forward of the rear axle.

Movie Cars

Many historical cars have been restored for use in the making of motion pictures. These cars are catalogued and identified by year and model. At right is a 1906 Sears, Roebuck car. This ancient vehicle, which looks as if it's in search of a horse, is a high-wheeler with solid rubber tires and double chain drive to the rear wheels. The opposed two-cylinder engine was cooled by air. Like many early automobiles, the body was of buggy-type design and a folding top was held up by two straps, attached to the front of the body. This car sold at $395, and Sears offered the buyer ninety days' free trial.

Directly below is a 1913 four-cylinder Reo. This was one of the first cars, after Henry Ford

built the Model T, to have the steering wheel on the left-hand side. This particular model had a three-speed gearshift lever extending through the floorboard in the center and operated by the right hand.

At lower right is one of the famous early Hudson racing cars built prior to 1916. The Hudson car first saw the light of day in 1909 when Roy Chapin and Howard Coffin, backed by Detroit department-store owner W. S. Hudson, decided to go into business for themselves. Both had at one time been associated with Ransom E. Olds.

Long Island Museum

Austin H. Clark operates the Long Island Automotive Museum in Southampton, Long Island, which houses over one hundred antique cars and trucks in several buildings. Shown below are but four of the ancient steam, gas, and electric buggies belonging to Mr. Clark's collection, in which are to be found famous and obscure makes of American and foreign cars, ranging from small machines of the late nineteenth century to powerful cars of more recent years. Special collections of the Ford and Pierce-Arrow lines are featured, as well as several early fire engines. The outstanding racing car on display is the famous Thomas Flyer which won the historic New York to Paris race in 1908. The museum workshop is constantly engaged in the restoration of old cars, and this interesting process can be viewed by the visitor.

1910 Simplex 50-hp. Speed Car

1911 36-hp. Pierce-Arrow

1911 Seagrave Hose Truck

1912 Moon Raceabout

Old-timers Today

It takes a good deal of time, patience, and skill to restore old cars as successfully as the examples on this page. Directly below are two photos of Pat Whittington's high-wheeler, which was manufactured by the Columbus Buggy Company in 1907. It had a folding top, but was slightly before the pushbutton era.

At lower left is a 1912 Studebaker-Flanders "20" which I'm proud to say I own myself. With R. A. Van Alen, standing at right, I drove the car in a Horseless Carriage Club Caravan from Los Angeles to San Francisco in 1950. The car is shown alongside a 1950 Studebaker. Each is an object of beauty, in its own way.

At lower right is Dr. Rafe C. Chaffin in his retored 1912 Studebaker E-M-F "30." This car has been in constant use by Dr. Chaffin in recent years and can be seen daily on the streets of Los Angeles.

Chicago's Museum of Science and Industry

One of the country's finest collections of skillfully restored antique cars is on display at the Museum of Science and Industry in Chicago: Left, an armored car built in 1898; directly below, a 1911 Brush on which a covered-wagon body has been installed; below, left, the back-seat driver's Stevens-Duryea (1904–1905); bottom, the Wheels of a Century Exhibit—left to right, a Rambler 1902, a Cadillac 1904, and a Stevens-Duryea with top up, 1904–1905.

The Restored and the Restorer

More beautiful examples of the restorer's art from the Chicago Museum: (*A*) a 1915 Electric Buckboard using bicycle wheels and designed primarily for children's use, although some were used by adults; (*B*) a 1913 Chicago Electric alongside a 1902 miniature electric runabout; (*C*) a 1910 McIntyre in the first stages of restoration; (*D*) a 1906 White Steamer being restored; (*E*) an 1893 French De Dion Bouton three-wheel steam car; (*F*) Maj. Lennox R. Lohr beside some of his collection—left to right, a 1911 Stoddard-Dayton, a 1913 Chicago Electric, a 1910 Milburn Electric, a 1910 Sears, and a 1900 Locomobile Steamer.

A

C

B

D

E

F

The Thompson Museum

The cars on this page are from the fine collection of restored automobiles in the Thompson Museum of Cleveland, Ohio, under the direction of curator Ruth Franklin. At upper right is the 1899 Baker Electric; directly below, the 1905 air-cooled Franklin. At center left is the 1905 Duryea; at center right, a 1908 Anderson. At lower left is a 1930 Rolls-Royce "P-11"; and at lower right, a 1909 Stevens-Duryea.

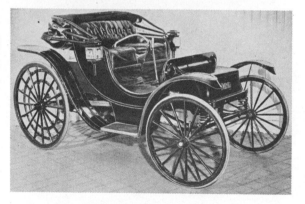

The Smithsonian Institution

In the National Museum at Washington, D.C., many famous cars are on display. Below, right, is the historic Patent Office model submitted to the United States Patent Office by George Baldwin Selden, in 1879, on which Patent No. 549,-160 was granted in 1895. This model is now exhibited in the National Museum. About 1905, a full-sized version of this vehicle was built as an exhibit for the court while the Selden Patent suit was under way. This court model is now at the Stevens Institute of Technology, Hoboken, New Jersey.

The photo at bottom, right, is of the original Duryea automobile built in 1893–1894 by Charles E. and J. Frank Duryea at Springfield, Massachusetts. It was operated on the streets of that city in September, 1893, with a friction drive and in January, 1894, with the present gear transmission. It has a one-cylinder, four-stroke, 4-horsepower water-cooled gasoline engine with make-and-break electric ignition. Up-and-down movement of the steering tiller shifts the two forward speeds and one reverse. The car's weight is 750 pounds.

The vehicle below, left, was one of four manufactured in 1897 by Ransom E. Olds of Lansing, Michigan. The first Olds gasoline car, which was destroyed by fire, was not really an Oldsmobile because it predated the name. The name Oldsmobile actually came into use when Olds organized the Olds Motor Vehicle Company at Lansing, Michigan, in 1897.

At lower left is the 1894 Haynes with a one-cylinder Sintz gasoline engine. It was first driven at Kokomo, Indiana, on July 4, 1894. The car was designed by Elwood Haynes and was built by Elmer and Edgar Apperson. The car was a gift to the Museum from Elwood Haynes.

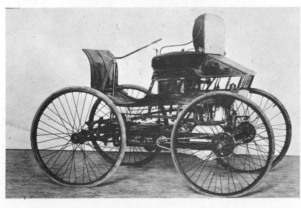

Smithsonian Specimens

At upper left is the 1898 Winton Gas Car, now in the collection of the United States National Museum, Washington, D.C. It was the first one of twenty-five Winton cars scheduled for production and was the first Winton sold. It has a one-cylinder gas engine and single-tube tires.

Upper right: This 1902 Franklin four-cylinder car had a transverse-mounted gasoline engine which was cranked on the right side. This car was the third Franklin manufactured and the first one sold. It was also put on display in the United States National Museum after restoration by the museum staff.

Alexander Winton, lower left, seated in his 1902 Winton gasoline racing automobile, known as "Bullet No. 1," now exhibited in the United States National Museum. Winton put his first car on the road in 1895 and was for a few years a dominating figure in the infancy of the car industry.

At lower right is a 1900 Locomobile Steamer. Locomobile was the pioneer manufacturer of steam vehicles, which bought the Stanley patents for a quarter of a million dollars.

The Immortals Restored

The first car to cross the United States under its own power is the 1903 model Winton now in the United States National Museum and shown at right. Winton himself, six years earlier, drove one of his first cars cross-country from Cleveland to New York. Winton was a determined Scotsman who had been a steamship engineer and a bicycle maker. One of his early models was among the first American cars with a steering wheel instead of a lever.

The photo reproduced at left, below, is a view of a quarter-size scale model 1907 Rolls-Royce (National Museum collection). This luxurious import from England was, and still is, one of the world's finest cars.

One of the outstanding cars in American automobile history was the 1912 50-horsepower Simplex shown at bottom and now in the Smithsonian. This model was one of the fastest cars then built in America; Simplex was a famous name in early American automobile racing. Double chain drive was used. Note the high location of the clutch and the brake pedals. The speedometer, kerosene lamps, and bulb horn are mounted on the side of the dash.

VIII. The Survivors

Any list of "surviving" automobiles must be somewhat
arbitrary. The second half of this book is devoted to
twenty-one such makes produced by companies that have
their roots in the pioneer era of the American automotive
industry and are still producing today. In some cases they
no longer make automobiles, but concentrate solely on
trucks. Certain makes were bought out by other companies with a resulting change in name. And of course
there are a number of healthy car companies producing
today which are not represented here because they have
entered the field relatively recently.

Autocar

Throughout the years the Autocar Company of Ardmore, Pennsylvania, manufactured well-known cars and trucks. Shown below, right, is the first automotive vehicle, No. 1, manufactured by the Autocar Company in 1897. Mr. Louis S. Clarke, founder of the company, is shown alongside the experimental tricycle which had a one-cylinder air-cooled engine and a differential. This photo, take in 1944, shows the restored tricycle, which weighed about the same as one of the front springs of a 1944 heavy-duty Autocar truck. This automobile curiosity is now in the Franklin Institute Museum in Philadelphia.

Below, left, is the 1898 Autocar which was the second vehicle built by Mr. Clarke in his Pittsburgh motor-vehicle shop. It was called a Four-wheel Phaeton. Steering was by lever. Full elliptic springs were used all around. Mr. Clarke restored this model to running order himself,

working at his home in Haverford, Pennsylvania, in 1950.

Bottom, right: This 1904 Autocar was advertised "to meet the demand for a beautiful durable Runabout built on the lines of the best touring-car practice." The engine was a two-cylinder horizontal opposed, developing 10 horsepower. Wheelbase was 70 inches; tread, 52 inches; weight, 1,200 pounds. This model was manufactured until 1906.

Early Shaft Drive

The Autocar's two-cylinder opposed engine with sliding-gear transmission and cone-clutch in the flywheel is shown above. Autocar was one of the first shaft-driven vehicles to be built by any manufacturer. There was no cover for the timing gears, and this engine had automatic intake valves.

At bottom is a 1901 Autocar with a two-cylinder water-cooled engine. This was one of the first shaft-driven Autocars. In December, 1951, it was driven all the way from the factory at Ardmore, Pennsylvania, to the Automobile Show in New York City. It is now on display at the Smithsonian Institution in Washington. Mr. Clarke of Autocar was one of the first to abandon chain drive and adopt shaft drive.

No Steering Wheel, 1906

By 1906 the Autocar had been improved and acetylene headlights and kerosene side lamps were available (below). The steering wheel had not as yet come into use by Autocar. However, the two-cylinder engine and shaft drive were excellent features. Directly below is a reproduction of the metal plate attached to all makes of automobiles that were licensed under the Selden Patent. Autocar, like almost all other manufacturers with the exception of Henry Ford, was licensed under the Selden Patent and paid royalties to the Selden interests. After 1911, Autocar devoted itself entirely to the manufacture of trucks, and it has been in this phase of the automotive business ever since that time, with considerable success.

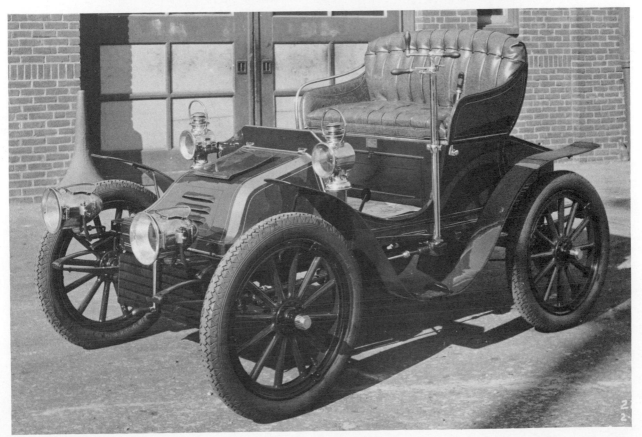

Three Trucks and a Car

One of the novel features of the earliest Autocars was the position of the engine under the seat. From 1908 to 1920, more than 30,000 two-cylinder Autocars of this design were made.

Shown at top right is a four-cylinder 25-horsepower Autocar Touring Car. This 1910 model, one of the company's last passenger vehicles,

sold for $1,750. At top left is a 1918 Autocar Truck used to haul supplies during World War I. Below, right, is a scale model of the 1921 Autocar gasoline truck which is to be found in the Smithsonian Institution. Below, left, is another 1921 Autocar model, this one a dump truck, also in the Smithsonian.

On September 10, 1903, a group of blacksmiths meeting at Flint, Michigan, collected $5,000 to start a state college of horseshoeing. On the same day, the Flint Wagon Works bought the infant Buick Motor Company of Detroit for $10,000 —and moved it to Flint.

Buick is the oldest division of General Motors, and the cornerstone on which the huge industrial empire is founded. David Dunbar Buick, a Detroit plumber, first made bathtubs. His process of annealing porcelain to iron is said to have helped make possible the white bathtub. Later he turned his attention to automobiles. Buick's first car had a two-cylinder opposed valve-in-head engine; but the inventor did not stay long with the company that still bears his name today.

Buick built sixteen cars in 1903 and thirty-seven in 1904. Late in 1904 William C. Durant, the "boy wonder" of Flint, and even then a well-known carriage builder, came into the Buick organization as general manager. . . . Below is an assembly plant in Jackson, Michigan, where Buick cars were manufactured for a short time. The Buick factory, at bottom, was in Flint when Durant was in control.

"When Better Automobiles Are Built" . . .

In 1908 Buick's famous "White Streak," the Model 10, became a sensation, and Buick produced a total of 8,820 cars that year. The company's progress was virtually assured from that time on. Such automotive geniuses as Charles W. Nash, Walter P. Chrysler, and Louis Chevrolet helped to operate the mushrooming firm while Durant turned his amazing organizing talents to founding General Motors in 1908.

Early in Buick history, someone conceived the slogan that was to become world-famous, and today it remains: "When Better Automobiles Are Built, Buick Will Build Them." The first slogan had an introductory phrase: "We build nothing but high-grade automobiles, and *when better automobiles are made, Buick will build them.*"

In the photo below, 1903 Model B, one of the first Model B's ever built. The car was driven by Walter Marr, who became chief engineer of Buick, and the passenger is Mr. Buick. The car

developed 22 horsepower from a two-cylinder opposed engine under the seat. At the top right, an early famous racing driver by the name of "Wild Bob" Burman is shown driving a Model 10 Buick Roadster in tests on a half-mile dirt track.

Early Driveaway

The top photo, taken in 1904, shows Buick cars being driven by Buick dealers through the streets of Flint en route to nearby towns. Below, left, is a view taken inside the Buick plant about 1906. Lathes were driven by overhead belts and the foreman, visible in the center aisle, wore a derby hat.

At the lower right is the concluding portion of the report made by the auditor, J. W. Wellington, in 1908, in which he stated that the Buick business was "in excellent condition and could be developed to give magnificent results." Mr. Wellington's typewriter stumbled badly but his foresight into Buick's future was correct.

what is ptobably the finest equipment in the Country for
the manufacture and sale of automobiles.

The busines as a whole is in excellent condition and can be developed to give magnificent results with
an extremely large factory output, a great volume of sales
and excellent profits.

Yours very truly

May 21, 1908 J. W. Wellington.

The Little White Buick, 1908

Of all the Buicks built, none was more famous than the Model 10, offered in various styles. The one below is shown with a single "mother-in-law" seat in the rear. This model won countless road and stock-car races, and Buick advertised it as "the most popular car in the world for women" as well as one that appealed to "men with real red blood who don't like to eat dust." The popular 1908 Model 10 spurred Buick production in 1909 to above 10,000 units.

At lower left is Buick's first valve assembly and carburetor, the latter described as "an improved automatic float-feed type insuring uniform action at every speed."

The Buick Model X Runabout (below, right), also 1908 and very similar to the Model 10, sported a carburetor (price $8.50) guaranteed to "start the motor on the first turn of the crank, give a speed of from 5 to 50 miles per hour in high gear, and give instant acceleration without skipping or 'choking.'"

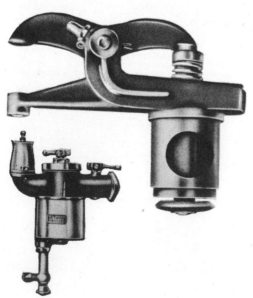

Buick Racing

For many years Buick competed in all sorts of racing events. Shown below are three Buick racing cars which were driven by such famous early-day race drivers as the Chevrolet brothers, Bob Burman, Eddie Hearne, Ewing Easter, and Louis Strang.

An early much-publicized Buick around-the-world car is pictured at the lower left in front of the Sphinx. At lower right is the start of a 1909 race in which three Buick cars (in foreground) competed. These Model 16 Buicks were extremely popular in all types of competition. "Wild Bob" Burman won the first 250-mile event held on the Indianapolis Speedway, in 1909, driving a Buick. While the first 500-mile race was held in Indianapolis in 1911, races for shorter distances were held there as early as 1909.

The Buick and the Airplane, 1908

In 1908 a Buick raced an early airplane, but unfortunately both driver and aviator are un-identified. Buick is given credit for having won this race, claimed by some to have been the first race between air and ground craft. Such stunts were cleverly used to publicize not only Buick but the whole industry.

Shown below is the well-remembered Buick Bug, which was driven by many well-known drivers in dirt-track races. This car had the unbelievable displacement of 622 cubic inches and a bore of 6 inches with a stroke of 5½ inches. Weight, 2,600 pounds; four-cylinder overhead-valve engine, 57.6 horsepower.

Chassis Manufacturer:	Buick Motor Division of Gen. Motors	Displacement:	622 Cubic Inches	Foot Brakes:	1 Contracting on Trans.
		Ignition:	Original-Bosch Dual (Magneto); Present Delco Dual (Battery)	Hand Brakes:	2 Expanding on Rr.Whls.
Address:	Flint, Michigan	Carburetion:	Schebler	Frame:	Steel Channel
Body Manufacturer:	Buick	Cooling:	Water. (Tubular radiator around cowl).	Spring Suspension:	Semi-elliptic
Body Type:	1 Pass. Racing	Lubrication:	Force feed & splash.	Wheels:	Artillery with discs.
Model:	Special "60"	Clutch:	Cone-leather faced.	Rims:	Firestone Demountable.
Engine Type:	4-Cyl.Cast in pairs.	Transmission:	Selective 3-speed, and reverse.	Tires:	32 x 4
Valves:	Valve-in-Head (push rod operated).	Final Drive:	Bevel Gear.	Wheelbase:	102-1/2"
Bore & Stroke:	6 x 5-1/2	Gear Ratios:	1st-7.43:1; 2nd 3.38:1; 3rd-2.25 :1; Rev. 9.68:1	Tread:	48-1/2
Horsepower, A.L.A.M.	57.6	Steering:	Wheel, worm and sector.	Weight:	2600 lbs.

Buick Experiments

Over the years, Buick has manufactured about every conceivable type of automobile, and Buick engines have at one time or another had two, four, six, eight, and twelve cylinders. Above, right, is an early enclosed Buick bus. At one time Buick also built a few trucks. Directly below is one of the first experimental Buicks, which appears to be a "mock-up" as an outline for future styling. This exact model never was produced. Rear passengers entered the tonneau by a back door, and the absence of the steering wheel indicates that the designer had not decided whether it should be on the right- or the left-hand side. Notice the wooden body, the square radiator, and wood artillery wheels with clincher tires.

The middle photograph at right is of a twelve-cylinder Buick designed by Chief Engineer Walter Marr. This model was never produced, but three experimental models were made. At lower right is an experimental Buick having a V-6 engine which likewise was discarded as being impractical. The Buick Eight has long been standard.

Buick Progress

The two-cylinder 1905 Buick shown at upper left had a two-speed planetary transmission with the two-cylinder engine under the body. Gasoline and water were carried under the hood. Gas headlights and the windshield were extras, as was the top.

At left center is the classy 1910 Buick four-cylinder closed car. At lower left is the popular light six-cylinder model built in 1916.

The flat-topped model at upper right is the 1921 Six Coupé with a permanent sun visor. By 1926 the Standard Six shown at right center was equipped with bumpers and windshield side-wings. Lower right: the 1930 four-door sedan.

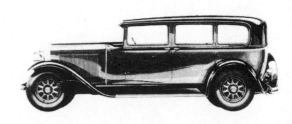

Engineering and Sales

General Motors engineers have constantly devoted their best efforts to assist Buick in engineering achievements that have kept it throughout the years one of the world's most popular cars. Shown below, left, is an early experimental Buick with Charles F. Kettering, inventor of the electric self-starter, at the wheel. Another engineer, W. A. Chrys, is the passenger, and they are testing the first Delco self-starter installed on a 1913 experimental-model Buick.

Shown at bottom is a Buick salesroom of the 1913 era. This Buick sales agency in Denver, Colorado, made the photo on the occasion of the first trainload of automobiles ever purchased by a Denver dealer. The agency had a balcony for customers desiring a bird's-eye view.

DOWNTOWN BUICK, INC., E. COLFAX AT LINCOLN, DENVER, COLO.

This photo made in our showroom in 1913 on the occasion of the First Train Load of Automobiles ever purchased by a Denver Dealer. Retail Value $162,120.00 — largest single cash shipment ever sent to Colorado to that date.

They are Buicks. Then as now, Buick Stability, Reputation and Service
MAKE BUICK SELL

Buick Tradition

The Buick ad for the brougham sedan (bottom right) appeared in 1924, and for many years the company had a unique radiator design which was a distinctive identification of the Buick car. The photographic portrait below is a rare shot of the car's inventor, David Dunbar Buick, who started the business on a shoestring in 1903. Very soon after the appearance of his first car, Buick had to sell most of his interest in the company.

Many employees have been with the Buick firm during most of its existence. In 1952 these six long-time Buick employees (below, left), all of them eighty years old or over, say farewell to Buick and prepare to leave the Flint plant for the last time. Their services ended on June 30, 1952, under the General Motors retirement plan. They are, left to right, H. E. Aris, eighty; D. G. Carroll, eighty; Charles A. Hendrick, eighty-four; Thomas W. Old, eighty-two; Henry Parish, eighty; and William Dixon, eighty. They are shown with a 1911 Buick which Carroll (seated behind steering wheel) helped build four years after he started to work at Buick.

24-SIX-51 BROUGHAM SEDAN

This is the finest example of coach design. Measuring 128 inches from hub to hub, with a long, low body of finest Fisher quality, and with its length accentuated by the tourist trunk rack and tires at the rear, it has that appearance of extreme length combined with close touring comfort which is so desirable in the special Brougham Sedan.

Motoring is a luxury in such a motor car. On the rear is a trunk rack of new design, with new protecting bars and buttons, and the rack is capable of accommodating a full-sized steamer trunk. The inside of the car is very wide and roomy and has the same deep plush upholstery as those Buicks designed primarily for social use. Thus the Brougham Sedan serves a double purpose.

This car has power to start and power to stop. The new Buick Valve-in-Head motor delivers ample power and speed for all purposes, and the Buick four-wheel brakes give a tremendous factor of safety. Its six wide plate glass windows all have patent window regulators, and the equipment is complete, even to the clock and the gasoline gauge on the dash.

Cadillac
Standard of the World

From the days of the single-cylinder Cadillac (below, left), which was the first model built by the Cadillac Motor Car Company in 1903 after the reorganization of the Detroit Auto Company, Cadillac has maintained throughout the world its reputation as a builder of cars of the highest quality. The first Cadillac had a single-cylinder engine with a copper water jacket. and a unique valve-operating mechanism.

In the early days, Cadillacs competed in many contests, and the company was quite bold in its advertising. The 1906 Cadillac ad shown below, right, cautioned the auto prospect not to decide about auto questions until he had read the Cadillac book entitled *The Truth about Automobiles and What It Costs to Maintain One*. Shown at bottom is the start of the famous Dewar trial in England which was won by Cadillac because of precision workmanship which enabled parts of three Cadillac cars to be scrambled and then used for reassembly. The test was made to prove the interchangeability of Cadillac parts.

In the good old days, 1903 and thereabouts, a man could plunk down $750 and drive away his own Cadillac. It took a lot more doing to lay your hands on $750 in that pre-inflation period, but nevertheless that price has a nice democratic ring to it. The 1903 ad at right is a pre-production teaser aimed at prospective agents who, if they don't "secure it *now*, will hie themselves to the woodshed a little later and gently kick themselves all over the place." (Gently, sir, we'll have no rough stuff. Perhaps you should be selling trucks.) The Cadillac economy ad (bottom, left) mentions "sworn figures by disinterested owners showing just what it costs to run their cars" to prove that their product "is the most economically operated car in the world today."

The original genius behind the Cadillac, Henry M. Leland, was a maker of marine engines in Detroit at the turn of the century. He was one of the backers of the Detroit Auto Company, whose chief engineer was one Henry Ford. Leland and Ford disagreed, mostly about Ford's motor, and Ford was discharged. Later the company was reorganized, given the name of Cadillac, and Leland became its first president. This sixty-year-old Yankee engineer set precision, rather than speed, as his company's goal. It is said that he learned the advantages of precision during the Civil War when for three years he was a toolmaker machining standardized parts for Union Army rifles.

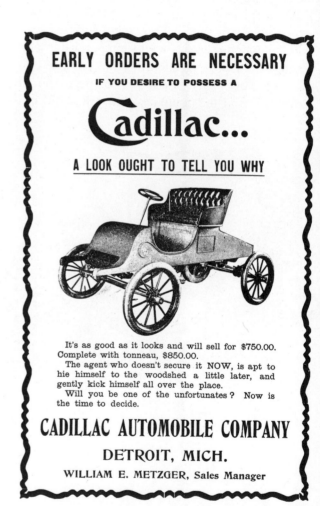

EARLY ORDERS ARE NECESSARY

IF YOU DESIRE TO POSSESS A

Cadillac...

A LOOK OUGHT TO TELL YOU WHY

It's as good as it looks and will sell for $750.00. Complete with tonneau, $850.00.
The agent who doesn't secure it NOW, is apt to hie himself to the woodshed a little later, and gently kick himself all over the place.
Will you be one of the unfortunates? Now is the time to decide.

CADILLAC AUTOMOBILE COMPANY

DETROIT, MICH.

WILLIAM E. METZGER, Sales Manager

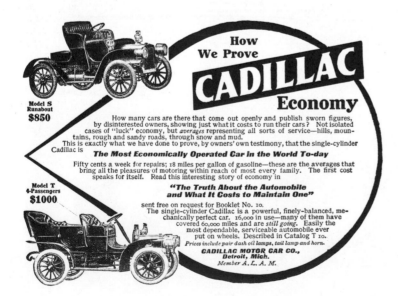

Model S Runabout $850

Model T 4-Passengers $1000

How We Prove CADILLAC Economy

How many cars are there that come out openly and publish sworn figures, by disinterested owners, showing just what it costs to run their cars? Not isolated cases of "luck" economy, but *averages* representing all sorts of service—hills, mountains, rough and sandy roads, through snow and mud.
This is exactly what we have done to prove, by owners' own testimony, that the single-cylinder Cadillac is

The Most Economically Operated Car in the World To-day

Fifty cents a week for repairs; 18 miles per gallon of gasoline—these are the averages that bring all the pleasures of motoring within reach of most every family. The first cost speaks for itself. Read this interesting story of economy in

"The Truth About the Automobile and What It Costs to Maintain One"

sent free on request for Booklet No. 10.
The single-cylinder Cadillac is a powerful, finely-balanced, mechanically perfect car. 16,000 in use—many of them have covered 60,000 miles and are *still going*. Easily the most dependable, serviceable automobile ever put on wheels. Described in Catalog T 10.
Prices include pair dash oil lamps, tail lamp and horn.
CADILLAC MOTOR CAR CO., Detroit, Mich.
Member A. L. A. M.

Three Old Beauties

The early Cadillac ad at right presented four different models ranging from $750 to $2,800 in price.

Below: The top photograph is of the 1905 Model D four-cylinder Cadillac. By 1909, the year that Leland sold his company to General Motors for four and a half million dollars, Cadillac had further established its reputation

with its Model 30 (center), which had the three-speed selective sliding-gear transmission. The photo at lower left is of the 1916 V-8, with electric lighting and a self-starter.

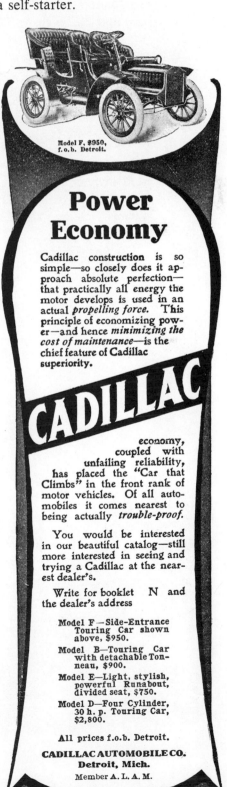

Model F, $950, f.o.b. Detroit.

Power Economy

Cadillac construction is so simple—so closely does it approach absolute perfection—that practically all energy the motor develops is used in an actual *propelling force.* This principle of economizing power—and hence *minimizing the cost of maintenance*—is the chief feature of Cadillac superiority.

CADILLAC

economy, coupled with unfailing reliability, has placed the "Car that Climbs" in the front rank of motor vehicles. Of all automobiles it comes nearest to being actually *trouble-proof.*

You would be interested in our beautiful catalog—still more interested in seeing and trying a Cadillac at the nearest dealer's.

Write for booklet   N and the dealer's address

Model F—Side-Entrance Touring Car shown above, $950.

Model B—Touring Car with detachable Tonneau, $900.

Model E—Light, stylish, powerful Runabout, divided seat, $750.

Model D—Four Cylinder, 30 h. p. Touring Car, $2,800.

All prices f.o.b. Detroit.

CADILLAC AUTOMOBILE CO.
Detroit, Mich.

Member A. L. A. M.

Interchangeable Parts, 1909

Prior to 1909 most cars were built from parts that were far from interchangeable. The conditions of the Dewar Trophy test conducted by the Royal Automobile Club of Great Britain were severe and the event was a dramatic one. Three

single-cylinder Cadillacs were sent to London where they were completely dismantled and their various parts thoroughly mixed up and tossed in a heap. With wrenches and screw drivers the only tools used, the three cars were then reassembled and tested immediately in a 500-mile run which all three completed with absolutely no trouble and at near record speed. At left are three photographs of the event: (top) various interchangeable parts; one of the Cadillacs in the process of being reassembled (middle); and the three cars on the street.

Below, right, a 1906 ad for two Cadillacs showing their wide price range in the early days: the Model M Light Touring Car for $950 and the Model H 30-horsepower Touring Car for $2,500.

Winter, 1913

This Cadillac ad appeared in *Automobile Topics*, 1913. "The handsome lines, the deep, soft upholstery, the yielding springs. . . ." It sounds like a living-room sofa.

We believe that orders for nearly every 1913

Standard
of the World

will be placed before winter is half over

The Cadillac has enjoyed many successful, many extraordinary seasons.

1913 is eclipsing all former successes.

Never in its history has Cadillac enthusiasm been so strong, so widespread, so pervasive as now.

The new car has literally taken the country by storm.

The handsome lines, the deep soft upholstery, the yielding springs, the riding qualities of almost velvety smoothness; the quiet engine of abundant power, the flexibility and the remarkable ease of control; the standardization of parts, the durability, the simplicity and the economy of maintenance; the practically 100 per cent efficient Cadillac Delco electrical system of automatic self-cranking and electric lighting, *now in its second successful year on the Cadillac;* these and almost countless other marks of distinction, stamp the Cadillac as a car which leaves nothing to be desired, nothing really worth while which a greater expenditure will procure.

The Cadillac production is large—15,000 cars for 1913—just one of the great elements which make possible the Cadillac car at the Cadillac price.

Before the new model was announced, dealers had contracted for this entire enormous output. They had also placed orders for several thousand more, our acceptance of these additional orders being conditional upon our being able by some means to supply them.

Without seeing the car or even its photograph, more than 3,000 individual purchasers placed their signed orders. They had confidence in the Cadillac car and in the Cadillac Company.

Four thousand of the new cars which have already been delivered have vastly intensified the early enthusiasm. They are proving that the confidence was not misplaced. They are confirming the wisdom of those who placed their orders in advance.

Nearly everyone you meet is—to use a common expression— "Sold on the Cadillac." There seems to be almost none left who are not convinced of Cadillac pre-eminence.

As we said at the outset: We believe that orders for nearly every 1913 Cadillac—including those for spring and summer deliveries—will be placed before winter is half over.

It behooves you, therefore, to arrange for as early a delivery as your dealer can give you.

By heeding this advice—given you in all sincerity,—you will avoid disappointment. You will also avoid the necessity of compromising on some other car—a proceeding which almost invariably results in an unsatisfied longing in the mind of the man who has once concluded that the Cadillac is the car he *wants.*

From Automobile Topics, 1913

STYLES AND PRICES

Standard Touring Car, five passenger	. . . .	$1975.00	
Six passenger car	$2075.00	Roadster, two passenger	$1975.00
Phaeton, four passenger	1975.00	Coupe, four passenger	2500.00
Torpedo, four passenger	1975.00	Limousine, seven passenger . . .	3250.00

All prices are F. O. B. Detroit, including top, windshield, demountable rims and full equipment

CADILLAC MOTOR CAR COMPANY, - - - - DETROIT, MICHIGAN

Closed Cars, 1914

By 1914 Cadillac advertising had taken on a dignified tone. A model of original design is this five-passenger sedan with a single door in the center of the body.

LANDAULET COUPE
(Three Passenger)
$2500 F. O. B. Detroit

CADILLAC ENCLOSED CARS

Here is provided the harmonious blending of the highest engineering achievement with the utmost in designing art and coach building skill.

The engineers have provided an eight-cylinder motor of superlative smoothness. The coach builders have provided a dignified and luxurious environment.

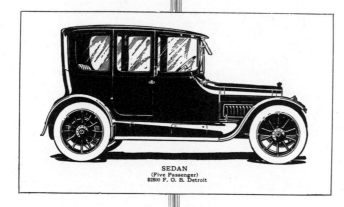

SEDAN
(Five Passenger)
$2800 F. O. B. Detroit

The liquid smoothness of these cars is supplemented by a sense of complete seclusion; the seclusion by a sense of rest and relaxation; the restfulness by a sense of unexampled ease and elegance.

Buoyant springs, deep soft upholstery. appointments in quiet good taste but still almost palatial—all of these soothing influences bring supreme comfort to mind and body, and leave you almost oblivious to the fact that you are borne along by mechanical means.

Special Enclosed Car Booklet on Request

LIMOUSINE
(Seven Passenger)
$3450 F. O. B. Detroit

Cadillac Motor Car Co. Detroit, Mich.

1919, 1923, 1928

Shown below is a 1919 V-8 touring car which was widely advertised by Cadillac's slogan as "The Standard of the World." In the center is a 1923 Model 63 Cadillac. This automobile featured four-wheel brakes, demountable rims, a permanent sun visor, and spare tire carried at the rear. Bumpers were still considered extra equipment.

At bottom is one of the most attractive Cadillac models ever made. This 1928 luxury convertible was one of the classic cars of the twenties. It had wire wheels, with spare wheels mounted in the fender wells; a large trunk on the rear, sleek and graceful lines. Nineteen twenty-eight was the year that Cadillac introduced synchromesh transmission.

Sixteen and Eight

While the powerful V-8 Cadillac has endured throughout the years since its inception in 1914, Cadillac has also experimented with cars having twelve and sixteen cylinders. Shown below is the wire-wheeled 1930 V-16, a large and luxurious car in its day. The V-16 Cadillac engineering and design were held in high regard by dealers and customers. Bottom of page: the 1932 V-8 Sedan, with a folding luggage rack at the rear; the spare wire wheels carried in the fender wells had metal covers. While the body is still rather conventional, the fender design indicates something of the early trend toward streamlining. In 1932, a year of deep depression, the total American car, truck, and bus output was at its lowest since 1918.

When the Chevrolet Motor Company was formed in 1912, operation was moved to a rented building on West Grand Boulevard in Detroit, where the Chevrolet brothers worked out the first Chevrolet model at the behest of William C. Durant. Actually, most of the preliminary work, carried on before the Chevrolet Motor Company was incorporated, was done on the second floor of the Schulte garage in Detroit, shown below, left.

The first Chevrolet-owned plant at Flint, is shown below, right; and at bottom, right, is an early experimental Chevrolet. Behind the car stand some of the men responsible for its development (left to right): Al Brush, an engineer; Louis Chevrolet (with white duster); William Little (in derby hat), who manufactured the Little car which was acquired by Chevrolet; an unidentified man; Etienne Planche, who worked with Chevrolet on the car; John Trumbull, an engineer who worked on the Little car; Frank Monroe, a Pontiac, Michigan, body builder; A. B. C. Hardy, general manager of Little Motor Car Company, who later became general manager of Chevrolet at Flint; and W. C. Durant, the genius of Chevrolet and for many years the guiding light of General Motors. Seated at the wheel of the car is Cliff Durant, son of Billy Durant, and his wife. The rear-seat passenger is unidentified. The car is the one developed by Louis Chevrolet of which a total of 2,999 units were built. The photo was taken in 1912. Below, left, Louis Chevrolet in helmet and goggles, taken in 1925.

The Baby Grand

The celebrated model Chevrolet Baby Grand Touring Car is shown in the two illustrations. Only three years after Durant had founded the company in 1911, there was talk of his Chevrolet's challenging Ford's Tin Lizzie.

1916

1914

The "490," 1916

The Baby Grand and the famous Chevrolet "490" were produced simultaneously for some time, but the "490" model became Chevrolet's car of quantity production. The "490" model was competitor of the famous Model T Ford, and Chevrolet's intensive sales and manufacturing efforts were thrown back of the "490" model. In 1916 the five-passenger touring car shown in the ad below was selling for $490. This model continued for some years without change. Equipment included a magneto and Prest-O-Lite tank, mohair tailored top, top cover and side curtains, an electric horn, ventilating windshield, and complete lamp and tool equipment, including a jack and tire pump. A $60 additional charge was made when the car was equipped with electric lights and starter. All in all, the "490" offered exceptional value and started Chevrolet on the way to becoming a sales leader in the automobile field.

The year 1916 was an eventful one in the auto world. Charles W. Nash left General Motors to start his own company; Cadillac was set up as a division of General Motors; Henry Ford bought the site for his huge River Rouge plant; and Studebaker added a touch of unaffected glamour to the annual automobile show by exhibiting a gold chassis.

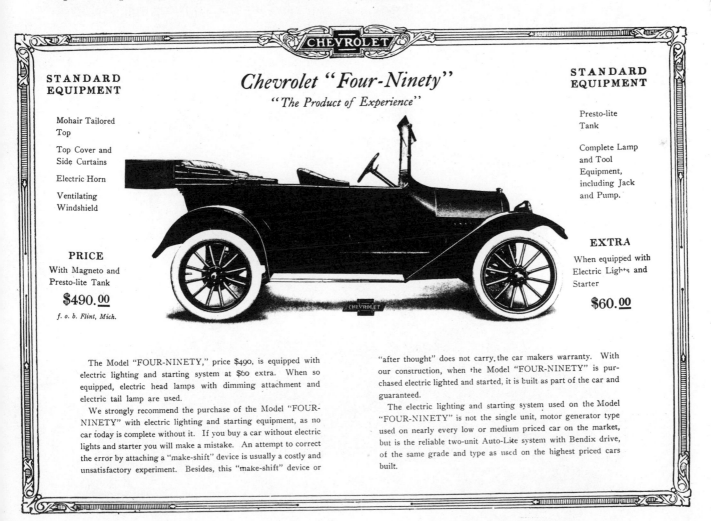

STANDARD EQUIPMENT

Mohair Tailored Top

Top Cover and Side Curtains

Electric Horn

Ventilating Windshield

PRICE

With Magneto and Presto-lite Tank

$490.00

f. o. b. Flint, Mich.

Chevrolet "Four-Ninety"
"The Product of Experience"

STANDARD EQUIPMENT

Presto-lite Tank

Complete Lamp and Tool Equipment, including Jack and Pump.

EXTRA

When equipped with Electric Lights and Starter

$60.00

The Model "FOUR-NINETY," price $490, is equipped with electric lighting and starting system at $60 extra. When so equipped, electric head lamps with dimming attachment and electric tail lamp are used.

We strongly recommend the purchase of the Model "FOUR-NINETY" with electric lighting and starting equipment, as no car today is complete without it. If you buy a car without electric lights and starter you will make a mistake. An attempt to correct the error by attaching a "make-shift" device is usually a costly and unsatisfactory experiment. Besides, this "make-shift" device or "after thought" does not carry the car makers warranty. With our construction, when the Model "FOUR-NINETY" is purchased electric lighted and started, it is built as part of the car and guaranteed.

The electric lighting and starting system used on the Model "FOUR-NINETY" is not the single unit, motor generator type used on nearly every low or medium priced car on the market, but is the reliable two-unit Auto-Lite system with Bendix drive, of the same grade and type as used on the highest priced cars built.

The Royal Mail

First Aid For Doctors

The doctor needs an all-weather car of high quality but low in cost and economical to operate.

Here it is.

Chevrolet Utility Coupé
$680 f. o. b. Flint, Michigan

Has a Fisher Body with extra wide doors, large plate glass windows with Turnstedt window regulators, cloth upholstery, comfortable, roomy single seat, and a mammoth rear compartment for instruments, sickroom supplies and luggage.

It is easy to handle, dependable every day in the year, and has ample power to contend with bad road conditions.

See Chevrolet First.

CHEVROLET MOTOR COMPANY
Division of General Motors Corporation
DETROIT, MICH.

Chevrolet's 1914 Royal Mail Roadster shown below was an attractive and dependable car. The standard equipment included gas headlights, kerosene cowl lights, top and windshield. Chevrolet's oval gas tank, mounted back of the seat, was also popular with other manufacturers, and the trunk mounted in back of the gas tank was an extra. At left is a 1923 Chevrolet ad calling attention to the fact that the Chevrolet Utility Coupé, at $680, was a dependable vehicle for the use of doctors. The car had a Fisher body with extra-wide doors, large plate-glass windows, cloth upholstery. The ad stated that "a mammoth rear compartment for instruments, sickroom supplies, and luggage" made it an ideal car for doctors' use.

In all, over three and a half million cars were manufactured in America in 1923, and almost a half million trucks and buses. This was over a million more cars than were produced the preceding year, 1922.

When Walter P. Chrysler (below, leaning on a 1937 Plymouth) decided to form his own automotive empire, he showed good judgment in purchasing in 1921 two going concerns, the Chalmers and the Maxwell. Although both companies dropped out of sight to make way for the new Chrysler, this shrewd entrepreneur acquired through them several hundred dealers. Chrysler had started his career in the automotive field working on the Buick under Charles Nash at General Motors in 1911. He quit G.M. (legend has it that he refused to sit around waiting for Durant to see him) and joined Willys-Overland in 1920.

An attractive 1906 Maxwell ad of the Detroit firm is shown at the right. The two-cylinder Maxwell was the first of the shaft-driven cars to become a top seller. The 14–16-horsepower two-cylinder model shown at the bottom of the ad had a two-speed planetary transmission, and the Maxwell Touring Car shown above was equipped with a 20-horsepower two-cylinder opposed engine. The 40-horsepower four-cylinder model, which the firm also manufactured, and the two-cylinder touring car had a progressive, sliding-gear transmission which made it necessary for the driver to pass through second gear when going from low to high or vice versa.

The "Maxwell" Touring Car

20 Horsepower, 2 Cylinders, Fully Equipped	$1,450.00
40 Horsepower, 4 Cylinders,	$1,750.00

"Maxwell" Speedster Runabout

14-16 Horsepower, Color Red, Price	$825.00
Very popular for all uses—a ladies favorite	

Howard Auto Car Company

Office and Sales Rooms:
404 WEST GRAND AVENUE

Warehouse:
131-133 WEST GRAND AVENUE

No Extras to Buy

A 1915 Maxwell advertisement for a $655 automobile is reproduced below. Notice the emphasis on true economy, both in original cost and in upkeep.

No Extras To Buy

Everyone about to buy an automobile is interested in cost—both first cost and after cost. Unless the car you buy really is completely equipped, its price does not at all represent the first cost.

The following is a list of equipment on the Maxwell Car with its approximate retail cost:

	Approximate Retail Cost
1—Electric Starting and Lighting System, Lamps, etc.	$95.00
2—High-Tension Magneto	50.00
3—Demountable Rims	25.00
4—Speedometer	15.00
5—Clear Vision, Double Ventilating Rainproof Windshield	12.00
6—Linoleum Covering for Running and Floor Boards	8.00
7—Anti-skid Rear Tires (cost difference over smooth treads)	5.00
8—Electric Horn and adjuncts	3.50
9—Spare Tire Carrier	3.50
10—Oil Gauge	1.50
11—Robe Rail	1.50
12—Front and Rear License Brackets	1.50
Total,	$221.50

If you purchase an automobile which lacks these features, you must add their cost to the price of the car if you want real automobile comfort. Deduct this amount ($221.50) from the price of the Maxwell ($655) and then you will realize what wonderful value is represented by the Maxwell Car.

Think of it—a beautiful stream-line car, built of special heat-treated steel, with a powerful four-cylinder motor; thoroughly cooled by a gracefully rounded radiator of improved design and a fan—sliding gear transmission—semi-elliptic front and three-quarter elliptic rear springs, making shock absorbers unnecessary—one-man mohair top—high quality upholstery, and ample seating capacity for 5 adults, really fully equipped for $655.

The high-priced car features mentioned, as well as the light weight of the Maxwell Car, account for the wonderfully low after-cost records of the Maxwell. The Maxwell is lowering all economy records for

    1st—Miles per set of tires
    2nd—Miles per gallon of gasoline
    3rd—Miles per quart of lubricating oil
    4th—Lowest year-in-and-year-out repair bills

See the new 1916 "Wonder Car" at the nearest Maxwell dealer's, and you will realize that it is the greatest automobile value ever offered.

Every feature and every refinement of cars of twice its price

Write for beautifully illustrated catalogue. Address Department A. L.

MAXWELL MOTOR COMPANY, Incorporated - - - - - - DETROIT, MICHIGAN

The Maxwell and the Chrysler, 1925

Walter P. Chrysler was one of the great names in the motorcar business. He worked with Durant, Ford, and the Dodge brothers, among others. He was with the Willys-Overland Company for a time and was also a vice-president of General Motors. The first car bearing his own name grew out of his purchase of Chalmers and Maxwell and made its first appearance in the middle twenties. Note the obvious similarities between the 1925 Maxwell Standard Sedan (top, right) and the 1925 Chrysler Six (below, left). When Chrysler took over the Maxwell in 1921 during the postwar slump, he renamed it "The Good Maxwell" (below, right), started right in to build better cars, and hired clever advertising

counsel. By 1922, he had built up Maxwell sales to 48,850 and earned a net $2,000,000 for the company. Chalmers, however, a subsidiary in the reorganization, lost $1,000,000; production ceased, and the car was written off.

America's Most Powerful Car

In 1928, the 112-horsepower Chrysler Imperial "80" (below, left) was advertised as "America's most powerful motorcar." The high-compression engine was called the "Red-Head" and was set in rubber mountings to help eliminate vibration. The Imperial "80" was one of the fastest automobiles made in the United States, and custom bodies were designed by such famous names as Locke, LeBaron, and Dietrich. Chrysler himself made some bodies in a special plant which he advertised as equipped "solely to produce these fine examples of coachwork." Prices ranged from $2,795 for the roadster to $6,795 for the LeBaron custom job.

In 1929 Chrysler was catering to the purchaser of the medium-priced car. The Model "75" Royal Sedan was a real bargain at $1,535. It is pictured in the ad below, right, before a 2,000-year-old Roman aqueduct and was said to have the "same charm of line and trustworthiness."

112 H.P. AMERICA'S MOST POWERFUL MOTOR CAR

With the new 112 h. p. Imperial "80" Chrysler now introduces into the field of finest motor cars a new modern note of simple excellence.

Powerful, graceful and fleet, this newest Chrysler emphasizes efficient simplicity in engine and chassis, and the charm of simple good taste in body and lines.

The new 112 h. p. "Red-Head" high-compression rubber-mounted engine—a marvel of clean design—is smooth and alert, easy to drive, maintain or control. No less pow-erful car can approach its flawless performance.

Graceful lines and luxurious custom bodies contribute importantly to Imperial "80" pre-eminence. In their simplicity of design and correctness of good taste there is not even a hint of that over-ornamentation sometimes mistaken for smartness.

Custom bodies are built by Locke, LeBaron, Dietrich, and by Chrysler in a special plant, acquired and equipped solely to produce these fine examples of coachwork.

Five body styles—Roadster, Town Sedan, 5-passenger Sedan, 7-passenger Sedan, Sedan Limousine—$2795 to $3495. Also in custom-built types by Chrysler, Dietrich, Locke and Le Baron, up to $6795. All prices f.o.b. Detroit, subject to current Federal excise tax. Chrysler dealers are in position to extend the convenience of time payments.

CHRYSLER IMPERIAL '80'

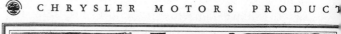

CHRYSLER MOTORS PRODUCT

CHRYSLER "75" ROYAL SEDAN (*wire wheels extra*), $1535

Many a Roman aqueduct still stands, after 2000 years, the epitome of strength and beauty. That same charm of line and that same trustworthiness of construction are reflected in the "arched-window" silhouette of the Chrysler today.

A Wealth of Strength
Beneath Its Classic Beauty

WHEN the first Chrysler overthrew traditions of motor car beauty and behavior, there was a twofold purpose for devising the new practices in design and construction it introduced.

Chrysler engineers determined to replace awkward bulk with lithe grace, stodginess with alert and zestful performance. Guided by the canons of classic art, they translated authentic principles of beauty into automotive terms.

The purpose of Chrysler's new design was also to enhance the utility of the Chrysler car.

The sturdy arches of the Roman aqueducts which have stood for 2000 years have been recognized as among the finest achievements of man's handiwork.

Not appearance alone directed Chrysler engineers to the arch of the aqueduct. The true arch is the acme of strength and rigidity, and so it was the Roman arch that served as the model for the construction of Chrysler windows and doors. Thus solidity and trustworthiness were concentrated at this point, masked by classic curve and flowing line.

It was not haphazard experiment and accidental achievement that developed Chrysler cars into symbols of grace in motion. They give greater value in performance as well as appearance because Chrysler engineers have never relinquished that twofold purpose of combining beauty with utility, swiftness with sturdiness, and luxury with dependability, in the proved integrity of Chrysler cars.

New Chrysler "75"—Nine body styles priced from $1535 to $2345. New Chrysler "65"—Six body styles priced from $1040 to $1145. Wire wheels extra. All prices f.o.b. factory.

Wrecks and Gags

This page has nothing to do with Mr. Chrysler, but it may lighten the atmosphere somewhat. Directly below is a picture of a badly scrambled 1901 Riker Electric, said to be the first auto wrecked in Pittsburgh. It was driven by one Robert B. King and was gently nudged by a streetcar. The cartoon at top, right, refers to the pneumatic bumperettes for autos invented for the protection of pedestrians by an Englishman, F. R. Simms, in 1916. Bottom, left: a photograph of perhaps the first wrecked Model A Ford which tested the Triplex Safety Glass Windshield. The windshield was bent 4 inches inward by the impact but remained intact, as shown.

Below, right, the manufacturers of Multibestos lining for brakes, in 1914, were willing to exterminate a whole family (in cartoon) under the wheels of a train to get across their message.

JIM JAMS AND HIS JABABOUT

Jim Jams he was a wise one
    And he lived in Cherry Lane;
'Twas an awful place to get to
    And a worse place to remain.
So to take his wife and fam'ly
    To the village which was far
He saved his hard earned dollars
    And bought a motor car.

One day as he was driving
    Down the long hill by the wall
The car it gave a plunge ahead
    And wouldn't stop at all.
He pushed hard on his service brake
    And pulled the lever back;
But the darn thing kept a-flying
    Till it reached a railroad track.

The four o'clock express was due
    And round the bend it whirled,
And it took Jim Jams and family
    To a better—fairer world.
Thus died poor Jim and in his fate
    One fact, it will arrest us,
How needless, if he'd lined his brakes
    With good old MULTIBESTOS.

DE SOTO

De Soto is one of the quality cars of the Chrysler line and was first manufactured in 1928–1929. Actually the first automobile to bear the name De Soto was manufactured in 1913 in Auburn, Indiana (left). However, Chrysler had no connection with this car and it did not survive the competition. Directly below is the first De Soto manufactured by Chrysler in 1928; 81,065 of these cars were sold the first full year. Center, right, is the 1930 De Soto Touring Car, the year steel model construction was begun by De Soto. At lower left is the 1931 four-door sedan.

A Durable 1929 Model

De Soto, most recent member of the Chrysler family, is a comparatively young automobile, but all of the Chrysler engineering data has been made available to De Soto, and many special innovations by Chrysler have been first tried out in the De Soto line. Below is a 1932 De Soto Phaeton with wire wheels and a rather classy touring-car body. At bottom, a four-door sedan model is shown, which was a conservative, practical, and economical car.

Shown at right is William A. Berry, a sixty-eight-year-old retired feed-mill operator who, with his seventy-two-year-old wife, in 1952, drove his 1929 De Soto from Denver, Colorado, to St. Johns, New Brunswick, on Canada's east coast, and then on to Washington, D.C. With 189,000 miles on it, Mr. Berry reported the car "runs like a top," that he traveled about 50 miles per hour on the highway, and got about 18 miles per gallon of gasoline. Mr. Berry had bought

the car from the original owner ten years before for $65. At that time the car had "only" 26,000 miles on it. According to Mr. Berry, the only mechanical work done on the car was a set of piston rings installed in 1948, at which time a reboring job was also done.

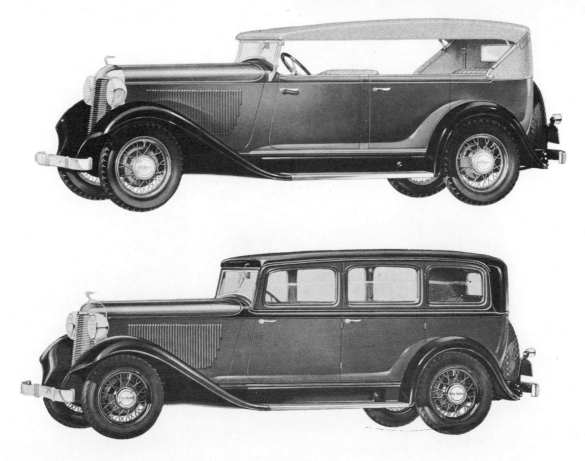

Dodge Brothers

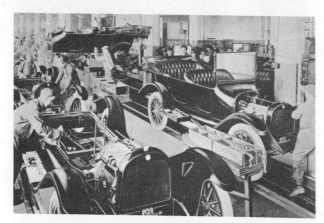

Horace and John Dodge got their start in the automobile business by accepting contract work from Henry Ford. But in 1914 at Hamtramck, Michigan, the Dodge brothers started their own automobile adventure, and it was an immediate success. Pictured directly below, their first assembly line had hand-operated chain hoists. At center, right, is the 1914 Dodge body assembly line, which, like those of all other car manufacturers, was an imitation of Henry Ford's original assembly-line idea.

The photograph at bottom shows one of the first auto test tracks in the United States. For many years the word "Dependability" appeared in almost every Dodge ad. Dodge cars were advertised only as *Dodge Brothers* Motor Cars, and the brothers set up this track to test each car before it was shipped from the factory. The test consisted of climbing and descending a steep incline to test engine and brake performance, and the slightly banked circular wooden track was used for speed testing.

All-steel Bodies

Dodge Brothers were pioneers in the manu-facturing of automobiles with all-steel bodies. Shown at left above is a 1916 Dodge Touring Car with a winter top. This top could be de-tached, but was not collapsible. Below, left, is one of the earliest trucks built in quantity pro-duction by any American manufacturer; this screen-side delivery unit was made by Dodge in 1917. Note the passenger-car chassis and wind-shield used in this unit.

At center right is the 1919 four-door Sedan with wire wheels. From their inception until the early twenties, Dodge cars had a different gear-shift from other makes, which caused some confusion for the driver accustomed to the con-ventional gearshift. At bottom is the 1925 four-door Dodge Sedan, equipped with balloon tires and steel disc wheels.

The Brothers

Both Dodge brothers, Horace (left) and John, were known as brilliant technicians in their field. In 1920 John died of pneumonia, and Horace followed him the same year. Yet as late as 1930 the Chrysler Corporation continued to use the name of the Dodge brothers in their advertising.

Note the location of the single door in the 1917 "closed car" (below, left). The 1923 ad reproduced below, right, pictures an $880 touring car.

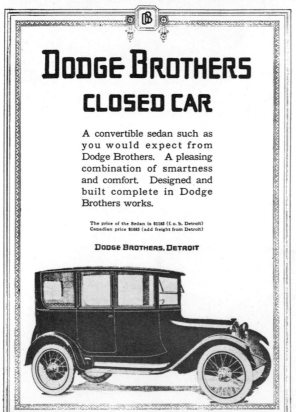

DODGE BROTHERS
CLOSED CAR

A convertible sedan such as you would expect from Dodge Brothers. A pleasing combination of smartness and comfort. Designed and built complete in Dodge Brothers works.

The price of the Sedan is $1185 (f. o. b. Detroit)
Canadian price $1685 (add freight from Detroit)

DODGE BROTHERS, DETROIT

QUICK ACTION BRAKES
EXTRA LARGE AND EXTRA SAFE

In the construction of Dodge Brothers Motor Car, every consideration has been given to the owner's safety.

This is particularly evident in the brakes, which, with their 14-inch drums and 2¼ inch lining, are appreciably larger than the average. The extra surface thus provided develops greater friction when the brake bands contract over the drums—and it is this friction which stops the car.

Connecting levers are designed to transmit the maximum of power with the minimum of effort. The slightest pressure on the brake pedal has an immediate effect. This pressure is distributed evenly between the two rear wheels by a highly efficient equalizer, which prevents skidding because it retards both wheels simultaneously.

And the brake bands grip evenly all around the drums. This protects the lining against irregular wear and enables the driver to stop quickly, quietly and safely.

DODGE BROTHERS

The price of the Touring Car is $880 f. o. b. Detroit

The Dodge Six

The Dodge Six (below) at $835 was quite a buy, although the depression in 1930 did not help its sales. By 1927, under the management of the Chrysler Corporation, many changes were being made in Dodge Brothers motorcars; for instance, the four-cylinder Dodge was on its way out because of public acceptance of six- and eight-cylinder cars.

DODGE BROTHERS
SIXES AND EIGHTS
UPHOLDING EVERY TRADITION OF DODGE DEPENDABILITY

At its astonishingly low price, the Dodge Six costs less and offers more than any other closed car in Dodge Brothers history. It gives you smooth, vigorous, economical performance. It gives you a Mono-Piece Steel Body—squeakproof, rattleproof and strong, with a low center of gravity that makes the car hug the road under even the most difficult driving conditions. You get good looks, too, and surprising roominess, and safe, positive, weatherproof internal hydraulic brakes. Above all, you get Dodge Brothers dependability—insurance of long and satisfactory service.

DODGE SIX
$835
AND UP, F.O.B FACTORY

Ford

Americans will long remember the name of Henry Ford (1863–1947). In the small machine shop pictured below in Detroit, Michigan, Ford built his first automobile in 1896 while he was working for the Detroit Electric Company. It was a small, crude two-cylinder affair and was constructed for experimental purposes only. Ford produced many early cars that did not become immediately popular, and he was hard-pressed financially until his famous $500 Model N car started him on his upward climb in 1905. He not only produced low-priced cars for the millions but established in 1914 the five-dollar minimum daily wage for an eight-hour day, which was almost unbelievable at the time. His critics claimed this radical move would bankrupt him, but just the opposite proved true: he attracted the cream of the labor crop and started operating three eight-hour shifts around the clock.

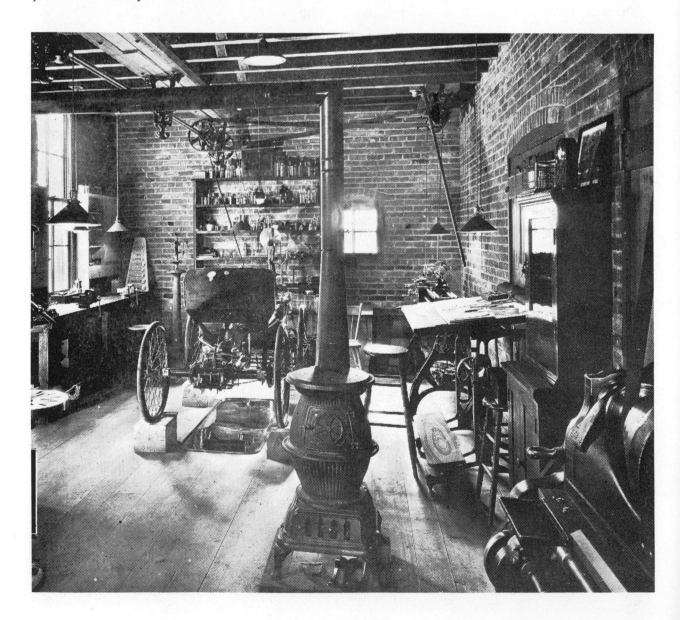

Ford Beginnings

Shown below is a two-story wooden building in Detroit which was the first Ford factory. By 1904 the well-known merchant John Wanamaker (a Ford dealer) advertised a world speed record made by Ford in his famous "999" racer. By 1905 Ford was producing the two-cylinder Model C, and in 1906 and 1907 he experimented with high-priced, heavy cars when he built the six-cylinder Model K which sold for $2,750. At this period in the auto industry, the six-cylinder Ford sold for about $2,000 more than the little single-cylinder Cadillac.

The photograph at bottom, left, shows Henry Ford in his garden. Ford was not only concerned with automobiles, but with many other ventures that he felt would promote the good of mankind. In the photo at bottom, right, Mr. and Mrs. Henry Ford are seen aboard his famous Peace Ship during World War I. Ford was intensely interested in promoting the end of the war and spent considerable amounts of money in his effort to do so. Although his peace mission ended in failure, its instigator remarked: "I would send another peace ship . . . if I thought that by doing so I could shorten the war a single day."

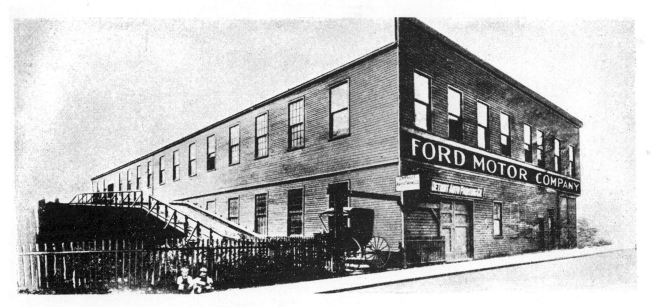

Mass Production

Below is an ad which appeared in British magazines in 1924 when Ford sales were already world-wide. In that year, Ford produced just under 2,000,000 cars. At bottom, left, a Ford tester sitting on a gasoline tank is testing transmission and brakes on a Model T. The rear wheels are revolving on a set of rollers, a method found to be efficient for testing purposes. At bottom, right, two assemblymen can be seen attaching a closed-car body to the chassis of a Model T. Ford was responsible for many improvements in automobile manufacturing methods.

The NEW FORD RUNABOUT

 A handy car this two-passenger Ford Runabout. Eminently suitable for the business man or commercial traveller desirous of increasing his field of action and to whom time is of great value. Exceptionally light on tyres, too.

This model might aptly be termed an ideal Sporting Car.

£105

On New Lowered Chassis
(At Works, Manchester)
Demountable Rims £5 extra.
Starter and Lighting Set £15 extra.

McKenna Duties
Ford Passenger Cars will be reduced in price when these Duties are discontinued. Refund of the whole difference will be made through the Authorised Dealer supplying.

Early Fords

Directly below is the Ford 1905 four-cylinder Model B car, with two-speed planetary transmission. Doors on each side of the top of the hood offered easy inspection of spark plugs and carburetor. At top right is the 1905 Model N Roadster. Ford shocked the automobile world by offering this car at $500. It was the first four-cylinder car to be sold for less than single-cylinder machines produced by Cadillac, Reo, Rambler, and Oldsmobile. Prior to the appearance of this Model N Ford, all these companies were leading Ford in sales each year.

The snappy Model R (center right) appeared in 1907, a year before the first Model T. At bottom, right, is the famous Model T of 1912. Front-seat passengers were offered the comfort of having front doors, although for several years the front door at the left-hand side could not be opened. This car had the renowned four-cylinder engine used by Ford until the fall of 1927.

It Had to Be Black

Although Henry Ford was a man of great ability and undoubtedly a manufacturing genius, he was stubborn, set in his ideas, and at times quite a controversial public figure. While other automobile makers were starting to offer cars in various colors, Mr. Ford made the startling announcement that "the buyer of a Ford car can have any color he wants, so long as it is black." It was many years before he gave in to the demands of his customers, dealers, and salesmen and agreed to use other colors as well.

Below, right, is a 1914 Ford Model T Coupelet which offered a folding top which today would make it a convertible. Note that the tires are bald as an eagle's head, with no tread design for any kind of traction. Below, left, is a 1922 Ford Model T four-door Sedan. This car had a permanent sun visor and a windshield with an adjustable upper half for ventilation. Although the car was equipped with a self-starter, Mr.

Ford made sure that its owner would be doubly protected in the event of starter or battery failure by retaining the hand crank in front. This model was referred to as the Fordor, a designation that Ford still retains for their four-door model. The four-cylinder engine was 20 horsepower, the wheelbase 100 inches, and tires 30 x 3 clinchers. The gas tank held 10 gallons.

At bottom is the 1926 Model T Ford Touring Car, which had been considerably dressed up with welded-steel wire wheels, windshield wings, bumpers, top boot, and balloon tires. This was one of Mr. Ford's last efforts to retain Model T popularity. American motorists were becoming conscious of sliding-gear transmissions and other improvements that were by now making the Model T somewhat obsolete in many ways.

Special Model T Coachwork

The era which was to become known as the "hot-rod" days was not to start in a big way until after World War II. But during the life of the popular Model T, there was a similar "hot-rod" movement, although it was not known as such. Hundreds of special bodies of all types and designs were offered to car owners. Many bodymakers offered their own custom-built jobs complete and ready to attach to their own chassis, while others offered them in "knockdown" form. Other bodymakers went after the business of the Model T owner who was interested in disguising his car. While every owner knew that the Model T had economy and endurance, some owners wanted to dress up their car to make it look like something more than just an ordinary Model T. Three such special bodies for Model T's are pictured below. Gadgets such as special mufflers, carburetors, and overhead valve units to increase speed and power were also available.

Build Your Own Body

"The Snappy Sport" (below) was the name of a body built for Fords in Chicago. Although it could be had without top and windshield at $60 or $97, the regular model was fitted with a "stylish mohair top and low racy windshield."

At bottom is one of many plans for car bodies made available to Model T owners by publishers of mechanical and automotive magazines. This one could be made from a set of full-size paper patterns and the body could be built without the necessity of laying up the car while the new body was being fitted. The maker claimed that the body changeover could be made in only 30 hours.

DOUBLE THE VALUE OF YOUR FORD WITH THIS BODY

F. O. B. Chicago **$97.00**

Without Top and Windshield
$60.00
F. O. B. Chicago

Painted FREE Stutz Red, Brewster Green, Blue, Orange or Black as desired.

H-W "SNAPPY-SPORT" BODY

AN IDEAL BODY FOR REBUILDING THE FORD

THE very latest and positively the most attractive Body offered to owners of Fords. Has graceful, streamline effect, as illustrated.

RIGHT UP TO THE MINUTE—LOTS OF SNAP

Fitted with stylish Mohair Top and Low Racy Windshield. Upholstered with high quality imitation leather with soft cushion seats. Has 20 gallon Gas tank with brass filler cap, extra large baggage or tool compartment in rear, latest style hood and radiator shell.

HINE-WATT MFG. COMPANY, Dept. "B" 180 North Market Street, **CHICAGO, ILLINOIS**

DEALERS

Here's Your Big Chance. Write today for Special Discount and Catalog.

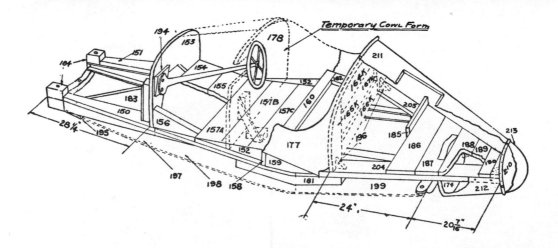

Dress-up Items

Thousands of ornaments, novelties, and gadgets were offered to owners of Model T's. Advertisers played on our natural desire to be different from, and better than, the Joneses.

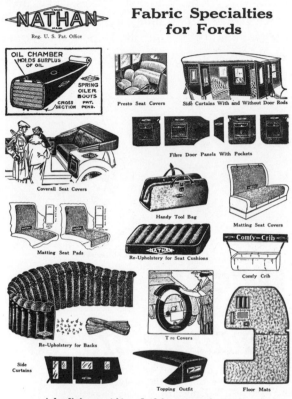

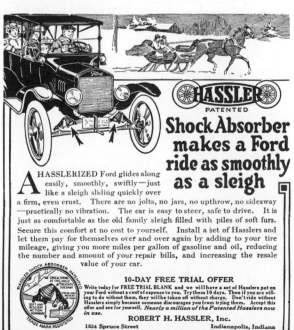

The Model T gas tank, until nearly the end of Model T production in 1927, was under the front seat. This inconvenienced occupants of the front seat. In 1920 the Kirstin Company devised a gadget to make the Model T owner happy; it is shown at left. Model T brakes came in for much criticism, and many improved brake units such as the 1924 Lincoln Dependable Brakes were offered to Model T owners.

Model T Jokes

Henry Ford's Model T, familiarly and affectionately known as the "Tin Lizzie," was honored by literally thousands of jokes. A few examples appear on this page, some more valuable for their historical significance than for their humor.

FILLING-STATION DIALOGUES

A Cadillac pulls up, and the driver say, "How far is it from here to Kansas City?"

"One hundred and forty miles," replies the man at the pump.

"Gimme twenty gallons of gas and a gallon of oil," says the driver. . . . And he drives on.

A Buick draws up, and the driver says, "How far is it from here to Kansas City?"

"A hundred and forty miles," replies the man at the pump.

"Gimme ten gallons of gas and a half-gallon of oil," says the driver. . . . And he drives on.

Along comes a flivver. It rattles up, the driver unwinds himself, gets out and stretches, and asks, "How far is it from here to Kansas City?"

"Oh, about a hundred and forty miles."

"Is that all? Gimme two quarts of water and a bottle of 3 in 1, and hold this son-of-a-gun until I get in."

WHEN TALK IS EXPENSIVE

"Hey, Bill, your doctor's out here with a flat tire, and he wants to know what it's going to cost him," announced the garage owner's assistant.

"Diagnose the case as flatulency of the perimeter, and charge him five dollars," came the answer.

THIS GENT WAS QUITE A WISECRACKER

A gentleman, who was visting his lawyer for the purpose of making his will, insisted that a final request be attached to the document. The request was, that the family Ford be buried with him after he died. His lawyer tried to make him see how absurd this was, but failed, so he asked the man's wife to use her influence with him. She did the best she could, but she also failed.

"Well, John," she said finally, "tell me *why* you want your Ford car buried with you."

"Because I never have got in a hole yet but what my Ford could pull me out," was the reply.

HERE'S A GOOD ONE TO PULL

"Here, boy," said the wealthy flivver driver, "I want some gasoline, and please get a move on. You'll never get anywhere in the world unless you push. Push is essential. When I was young I pushed, and that got me where I am."

"Well, guv'nor," replied the boy, "I reckon you'll have to push again, 'cause we ain't got a drop of gas in the place."

HERE'S A GOOD ONE ON HENRY FORD

A part of a noted magician's act is to make a horse vanish. That's nothing, though. Look at Henry Ford!

HEY! HEY! GIT HOT!

Filling-station Man: Yer car needs gas, Mister.

Mr. Grouch (who has stopped for Free Air): Say, that flivver had five gallons of gas day before yesterday, and that's every darn drop its going to get till tomorrow.

THIS AIN'T NO LIE

The guy who owns a secondhand flivver may not have a quarrelsome disposition, but he's always trying to start something.

WHY THE SISTER GOT HAPPY

In one of the small churches in a country town the pastor took for the subject of his sermon: "Better Church Attendance."

The parson held forth on the theme that the automobile has taken more people away from church than any other thing. He concluded with the exclamation:

"The Ford car has taken more people to hell than any other thing I can mention."

Whereupon an old lady in the congregation began to clap her hands and moan:

"Glory to God! Praise the Lord!"

"What's the matter, sister?" asked the parson.

"A Ford never went any place that it couldn't come back from, so I reckon all them folks in hell will be comin' back some day. So praise the Lord!"

"BOYS, SHE'S SOMEBODY'S OLD LADY," WEPT CHARLEY

An old country woman and her small son were driving to town when a clanking flivver bore down upon them. The horse was badly frightened and began to prance, whereupon the old lady leaped down and waved wildly to the flivver driver, screaming at the top of her voice.

The driver stopped his Ford and offered to help get the horse past.

"That's all right," said the boy, who remained composedly in the carriage, "I can manage the horse. You just lead Maw past."

THIS WAS IN ILLINOIS, SIX YEARS AGO

Flivver Driver: "Do you know which road goes to Chicago?"

Country Boy: "No."

Flivver Driver: "Do you know which road goes to Joliet?"

Country Boy: "No."

Flivver Driver: "Do you know which road goes to Wheaton?"

Country Boy: "No."

Flivver Driver: "You don't know anything, do you?"

Country Boy: "Yes, Sir. I know I'm not lost."

Ford Rhymes

Model T versifiers were not to be outdone by the jokesters. Almost every magazine printed sentimental or humorous verse about Henry's favorite creation. The three immortal ballads below won't appear in any anthologies, but they served a worthy purpose.

LOOK AND LISTEN

It has been said that money talks,
  And as I look abroad
Cash says with unanimity,
  "You'd better buy a *Ford*."
Thus popularity proclaims
  A nation's happy choice,
There's no disguising auto names—
  "A *Ford!*" shouts money's voice.

THE BIG CAR'S LAMENT

I wish I wuz a little Ford
  A-runnin' right along;
I wouldn't need to wheeze and sigh,
  I'd sing a different song.

To me the fact of bein'
  A big car is a fright;
I don't care if I do look fine,
  I never feel quite right.

An' when a Ford goes whizzin' by,
  Great tears most always drop;
For where the Ford can go right on,
  I'm almost sure to stop.

I stick in mud, I don't like rain,
  I can't pull up the hills;
Oh! I could sit here all day long
  An' tell you of my ills.

An' so I wish I wuz a Ford,
  Then I need never worry,
For they go back and forth each day,
  Without such needless flurry.

So just remember when you wish,
  To be so big and grand,
It's not the looks that count so much,
  As do the pluck and sand.

"C. L. H." vs. "H. C. L."

Just think of *me*, now, if you *can*,
Proud possessor of a Ford *Sedan:*
From "Cheap-John-Gang" I've gotten out
As owner of—"Just a *runabout*."
I'm here to state she's got some class,
All closed in—with so much glass;
A speedometer t' tell how fast
The poles and things are flying past.
Upholstered seats, electric lights,
To see your way about at nights
And shock absorbers, if you please,
Which makes it ride with so much ease
Wou'd think yourself upon the seas
Or—wafted on the zephyred breeze
And ev'n that *it* had *just* been grease(d).
A motor-meter, out in front,
Is, by no means, a "one horse" stunt
Which tells you when your motor's hot
And lots of other "Tommy-Rot."
Radiator of nickel plate,
With headlight rims in same state
And, like all other swell 'mobiles,
She's fitted with white wire wheels;
The lights burn "bright" or switch to "dim,"
Clock and "dash light"—make it "trim."
The *realest* thing this *sedan's* got,
Which keenly touched a "tender spot,"
'S the greatest thing about the car,
At least—I think—it *so*, by far,
Since t' *cranking*—Fords I've been —martyr
'Till a Liberty self-starter
Eliminates the toil and strife
That "took the j-oy out of life."

—But—

My *old* "Liz"—was a good old Ford;
She went all day to pay our board
And, when the daily toils were o'er,
She added to our *pleasures* more
Than any car we ever had—
So to part with "Liz" made us sad
Save when we'd think of what she cost,
Three-fifty-nine—'twas nothing lost
To let 'er *go*—in fact—'twas thrifty;
They "took 'er home" for just *four-fifty*.
Yes, we let 'er go and there did leave 'er,
Got the "dough"—and "Sedan Fever."

And *now*—we're looking forward to
Just lots of pleasure, as we go
Out riding in the afternoon,
Instead of—as if just to "spoon"
We'll take our *friends* and ride 'em 'round,
Even up for their "grub" we've ground,
Being invited out to dine;
We think it's fair, just simply fine,
Hearing their merry laughs and "prattle"
Instead of hearing "Lizzie" rattle.
We'd surely say this plan is *good*
If—it provides sufficient *food*;
Reduce *our* COST OF LIVING—My!
Our *friends*—the "COST OF LIVING HIGH."
Invite us early, 'void the rush
And save us from our milk and mush
Since starting keeping house last fall
That's all we have—that's all— that's all!
It's "milk and mush"—or—"mush and milk"
And 'course I swear—"It's fine as silk."
We *hope* there'll be a likely bunch
Who'll have us out to eat their lunch
We're trusting, though, they'll far exceed
Their luncheon bids—with those we need;
While riding 'round to hear 'em "spiel"
"*Do* come—and take an evening meal";
'Cause morns and noons I am not "strong"
But—after "going" all day long
The *dinner bell's* the sweetest song;
To 'vite us *then*—You can't go wrong.

As said before, "Miss Lizzie Ford"
For several years—paid our board
We're hoping *now*—that "Mary Ann"
'S a *food-producing*—Ford Sedan!!!!

RICHARD P. WINSTON

Versifiers, 1920

These two auto poets were enthusiastic about Henry's product in 1920. . . . The Ford pictured below is a 1931 Model B, last of the four-cylinder Fords. A few were built in 1932.

OMAR, A LA FORD

Now the New Year, surviving old desires
The thoughtless soul to his Ford retires
Where oily waste is scattered 'round about
And tools; and then under the heap perspires.

Come, fill the tank and fix the broken spring,
Your worn-out clutch into the garbage fling:
This car of thine hast but a little way to roll
And then you'll ask the wrecker what price 'twill bring.

Whether filled with distillate or gasoline,
Whether the rusty tank be filled or lean,
The stuff is costing drop by drop,
My purse is slowly sinking, bean by bean.

For some we owned, the newest and the best,
That in the fact'ry withstood each test,
Have proved the lemons of our lives
And back to the agent gone with praise supprest.

We'll make the most of what we have to spend
Before we, too, to the bankrupt's court descend
Dust to the dusty, but no dust we'll take.
Sans hat, sans coat, sans driver—what an end!

Into this old Ford, and why not knowing;
Gullible and fresh as any greenhorn, blowing
All about it. My money gone to waste
I know not whither—and the debt growing.

What, I am asking, made me do this thing;
And, I yet am asking, why keep this thing?
Oh many an hour of bursting brain
Must pay for this wild, wide wandering.

Once I remember stopping by the way
To help a friend and hear him furiously say,
"This all-abominated thing of painted tin
I'll scrap, nor ride another mile this day!"

And have not perspiring drops of old
Down man's impervious brow down rolled
When changing clincher rims of steel
Which by that wrecking pirate last were sold.

Each morn a thousand curses brings, you say;
Yes, for where's the gas of yesterday?
And this first trial spin that tests the car
Will surely take my home and purse away.

Well let it take them, what have I to do
With simple comforts and a house for two?
Let the butchers bluster as they will
Wifey, or grocers call for cash—heed not you.

With me along the road where wrecks are strown
And parts, and battered corpses thrown;
Where undertakers and their hopes are met
There, pieces of this car will soon be known.

A brawny son of toil beneath the car,
A wrench, a kit of tools, a sturdy bar
Beside him, sunken in the muddy ground;
Oh Ford, what a bally elephant you are.

Some for Cadillacs and cars of price, and some
Sigh for the bright-hued models yet to come;
Oh take my Ford and let the others go
I'll sell my interest for a tiny sum.

Think on this antique battered thing of junk,
In which our petty fortune we have sunk,
How owner after owner in his wrath
Rode his destined hour, then sold for junk.

Hot perspiration froze on my brow,
    My right arm was spent with woe,
For the traffic was stalled behind me
    And my flivver refused to go.

H. L. AUSTIN

WHERE FORDS GO BY

Let me move from the bustling highway,
    A lonely byroad will do,
Through a land of swamp and quicksand,
    Where only the Fords get through.
In a cottage there in the maples,
    Contented I'll be evermore;
For I feel the world's growing better—
    Where the Fords go by the door.

While other cars passing my cottage
    Are ditched, or something goes wrong,
They seldom grow weary of waiting
    For Fords to tow them along.
It seems that there's always one coming,
    Like the one rattling past them before,
And that's why I never get lonesome—
    Where the Fords go by the door.

The faint little purr of the motor,
    And tuneful honk, honk, as she goes,
Seem to lure my respect, and it follows,
    Like the cloud of gray dust that it throws.
And that's why I never get weary,
    Away from the great city's roar,
For I feel the world's growing better
    Where the Fords go by the door.

FRED KELLER DIX

G.M.C. trucks are manufactured by General Motors Corporation and are the successors of the Grabowsky and the Rapid. Shown below is a 1903 Grabowsky Power Wagon which had many unique features, some good and some bad. A special talking point was the removable power plant which pulled out like a drawer so that no time was lost for engine changes; inspection could be made quickly and easily without bending, crouching, or crawling.

The 1903 Grabowsky ad below shows the easy way in which the Grabowsky engine could be removed, and in the upper corner, an illustration of what Grabowsky claimed was the old way, where the power plant was inaccessible and it was necessary to crawl under the car to repair the engine.

If you study the fine print in this ad, you will be reminded that at this time—1903—Grabowsky was competing not so much against other trucks but against the old four-hoofed enemy, the horse. "The power wagon will do the work of three or more horse-drawn wagons—and do it better and cheaper."

Three Early Wagons

Rapid commercial cars were built in Pontiac, Michigan. The ad directly below for "commercial cars" mentions trucks, buses, fire-hose wagons, and hospital ambulances. In 1903, Grabowsky Power Wagons (ad at the right) offered enticing profit possibilities for any person entering the sightseeing field. Seen at the bottom is a skillfully fashioned scale reproduction of a 1912 Model S G.M.C., one of several used at that time by the Chicago *Tribune*.

Earn Up to $800 a Month

Many are making this much and more with *one* Grabowsky Sight-Seeing Car.

We have figures to *prove* that Grabowsky Sight-Seeing Cars yield larger profits than almost any other business requiring the same capital.

Men who are shrewd see the money-making possibilities of this proposition the minute it is laid before them.

Let Us Help You

Our plans for organizing and operating companies in rural districts and large cities make this a *safe* business for *anyone* to go into. We explain every detail—nothing is left to chance. You don't need to be an expert mechanic to manage a Grabowsky. Its simplicity is matchless. With a Grabowsky you can be your own boss—work in the open air—choose your own hours.

Mechanically Correct

The Grabowsky is a practical car—is always dependable. It has many *new* and exclusive features,

including a Removable Power Plant, which pulls out like a drawer, ready for instant adjustment and inspection. Other special features are hardened steel bushings, unique condensing radiator, original brake system, etc. Mechanical perfection means low maintenance cost.

Send for full information regarding the Grabowsky Sight-Seeing Car. Let us show you how you can start a highly profitable business with moderate capital *right in your own town.* Write today.

GRABOWSKY POWER WAGON CO.
111 Champlain Street   Detroit, Mich.

Grabowsky
Power Wagons

Rapid
Commercial Cars
Pay For Themselves In One Season

Hundreds of people have bought Rapid Passenger Cars as an investment, and all have found them wonderfully profitable. In most cases the car paid for itself the first season. A Rapid Passenger Car can always find profitable business at summer resorts, hotels, country clubs, in sight-seeing service and cross-country transportation

We make trucks, busses, fire hose wagons, hospital ambulances, and anything special desired.

N. B. HENRY, Sales Mgr., Rapid Motor Vehicle Co.
107 Rapid Street, Pontiac, Mich.

We have some excellent open territory for Agents who own a Garage.

The Horse's Low Morale

This 1910 Rapid ad tells of the remarkable performance of a Rapid truck in the 1910 Glidden Tour, pointing out that "hot and cold weather are demoralizing to a horse." The auto world's broadside against the Old Gray Mare was reaching its peak.

Remarkable Performance of a Rapid Truck

No Commercial Motor Truck except the DEPENDABLE "RAPID" would have dared the extraordinary trip in covering the Glidden Tour of 1910, **an endurance run of over 3,000 miles** over the worst roads in the world. The RAPID, being "BUILT FOR BUSINESS," has shown its supremacy in the Commercial Field of the Automobile Industry by this most gruelling test.

As in past years, we have again CHALLENGED every maker of motor trucks in the most exacting endurance run in the history of the industry, and **thrown down the gauntlet** to any and every maker to duplicate the great feat performed by the **perfected Rapid Motor Truck.**

We do not expect—and reasonably so—that our challenge will be accepted—for no other Commercial Car **is built or will be built,** by such men as are back of the Rapid.

The Rapid Motor Vehicle Company is the Pioneer Company in the Commercial Branch of the Automobile industry, and as such, have held the lead for ten years, **and intend to keep it.**

On the 1910 Glidden tour, over the worst roads, steepest and longest grades in the world, the Rapid Truck, loaded with over a ton of miscellaneous baggage and carrying five people, most of the way, has proven to be the **Marvel of Automobile construction.** All endurance runs of the past sink into oblivion alongside of the 1910 Glidden. Every touring car driver on the run says so, and wonders at the prowess and ability of the "Rapid" truck to run strong and come into control with flying colors, leaving behind it—**Down and OUT**—some of the best makes of pleasure cars. That is what the "Rapid" truck is doing right along, with cars in the Commercial class. There are **many derelicts** of other makes, but **none of the Rapid.** They are built right, and to last under the most unfavorable usage, and furthermore, are backed by the brains and capital to make them the best. A visit to the plant at Pontiac, Mich., will give you further assurance of the absolute dependability of the "Rapid."

Hot and Cold Weather are Demoralizing to Horses

Waiting for the other fellow is a losing game. To continue the archaic, inhuman, expensive method of transporting merchandise with horses, is the height of foolishness.

What the Automobile industry has done for the Country, the Rapid commercial car will do for you—"Build you up."

The success of your business depends upon quicker and dependable service—say nothing of the saving in dollars and cents, assured by the "Rapid" Truck.

The initial investment in a Rapid Truck is nothing when compared with the saving it affords; and the extra service obtained.

We have data, showing delivery cost in over 100 different lines of business enterprises, which is free to you. Write us to-day what constitutes your horse and wagon equipment and we will **show you,** that a "Rapid" truck will save you 33⅓ to 50% on your delivery cost—or no sale.

The Rapid Commercial Car is made in the largest plant in the world, backed by unlimited capital; and the brains of experts. Could you ask for more? You want the data we have, for it is not only interesting, but tells a story of how to save money that is convincing. **Write to-day for Catalogue G, and Book of Wonderful Tales.**

RAPID MOTOR VEHICLE CO.,
904 Rapid Street, PONTIAC, MICHIGAN

Pioneer builders of Commercial Motor Cars in America—Licensed under Selden Patent.

Trucks for World War I

During World War I, General Motors trucks gave excellent service in many branches of the government. Directly below is a G.M.C. truck with a special panel body. This body was made available in different versions by many body builders. In the early days of G.M.C. trucks, only the chassis was available for those who desired to build special bodies. At bottom, right, is a 1917 G.M.C. army ambulance equipped for Red Cross service.

Tractor and Tank Trucks

Shown below is one of the first G.M.C. tractor trucks with the enclosed cab for driver comfort. Notice the I-beam drop front axle, the starting crank and solid rubber tires. At bottom is a famous 1929 2-ton G.M.C. Tank Truck. This truck was driven by "Cannonball" Baker of Indianapolis in his famous speed run with a capacity load from New York to San Francisco. It was powered with a Buick six-cylinder engine,

and its capacity was 2 tons. Notice the extra spotlights for night driving.

This same Cannonball Baker claimed to have made some 118 trips from coast to coast in his automobile and motorcycle record trials. For years he held a number of speed records from the Atlantic to the Pacific, once driving cross-country from New York to Los Angeles in 53½ hours in 1933

HUDSON
MOTOR
CARS

One of the founders of the Hudson, Roy Chapin, started out as photographer and odd-jobs man for Ransom E. Olds. With Howard Coffin, an engineer, and W. S. Hudson, a Detroit department-store owner, he started the Hudson Motor Car Company in 1909 with stock subscriptions for $60,000 and about $15,000 in cash.

The 1910 Hudson "20" Roadster shown at upper right was a remarkable automobile, and popular in its day. The first 1909 Hudson, shown just below, had a four-cylinder engine, a strap

over the hood, and gas headlights. This car was apparently a test model, as it had no fenders and a step instead of a running board. Below, left, is a sketch of the 1912 Model "33" four-cylinder Hudson Torpedo. The Hudson at bottom right is a six-cylinder 1914 Model "54" Phaeton.

"The Road Cruiser"

Ready—the 1916 Hudson

This deals with the new-type Hudson, which has become in two seasons the most popular class car in the world.

It announces the 1916 model, with some vast advances, on a car which seemed beyond improvement.

New Price, $1350

First comes a new price. We have made another $200 reduction, due to a trebled output.

Only 20 months ago this new-type Hudson startled Motordom with a price of $1750. It was the first Six to sell under $2000.

The amazing demand brought the price on the next model down to $1550. Now the latest model sells for $1350. All due to the car's popularity.

Note that this price buys a higher-grade car than was ever built before it. The great feature of this car is its lightness. It weighs one-third less than the old-time Six. That weight reduction meant better designing, better materials, greater refinement.

So this Hudson, which now sells for $1350, really created a new standard of quality. And it typifies in high degree the new idea of class.

The growth in Hudson's sales from 1910 (4,107 cars) to 1914 (7,199 cars) was slow for the automobile business.

In early 1916 the Hudson Road Cruiser (shown at left) was popular. But the Hudson that made the greatest name was the Super Six, first brought out in 1916. Shown directly below is King Rhiley of Oshkosh, Nebraska, who won the 1921 Pikes Peak Race in a Hudson Super Six. At lower left is the 1916 Super Six seven-passenger Phaeton. This car offered many innovations, including a high-compression engine (high for the year 1916), and its performance delighted thousands.

Hudson's Runabout Landau, 1918

This 1918 two-seater was designed to appeal to everyone: professional men, women enthusiasts, cross-country tourists, and mountain climbers (of the automobile variety).

The Hudson Runabout Landau

—if you've been looking for a smart, semi-closed, two passenger car, here it is—on a Super-Six chassis—

Here is an adaptable, economical model for the driver who needs a two-passenger car and wants it attractively distinctive at all times.

With the top back and windows dropped, you have a perfect roadster. Top up, as in the illustration, your car is snug, compact, ready for any season or weather.

For professional men, the Runabout Landau is ideal. Women enthusiasts pronounce it delightful. Its graceful lines, low swung body and trim weather-proof top make a strong appeal to the particular taste. The pleasing variety of colors—beige, or gray, two shades of green, the top in Burbank or black leather—gives ample opportunity for individuality.

And it is a Super-Six—a 1918 Super-Six. You who have followed automobile development for years know the proven power and endurance the Super-Six possesses. You know that the happy experiences of your friends who own Hudsons are

backed up by two years of deliberate efforts to find the limits of Hudson Super-Six endurance by races, trans-continental touring, mountain climbs. You know too that Hudson engineers have taken advantage of all this experience to add every possible refinement, every possible improvement in detail.

All this is summed up in the chassis of your Hudson Runabout Landau—just as it is in the nine other Hudson Models—all fine Super-Sixes. This sum total means for you not only the style of car you want but a car which you can drive for years free from worry over the increasing curtailment of automobile production; with a minimum of concern over the increasing shortage of expert service men. The Hudson Super-Six is essentially a war-time automobile.

But to get your Super-Six—act promptly. Even now you will be fortunate if you do not have to wait. Anticipate your future needs by placing your order at once.

Hudson Motor Car Company   Detroit. Michigan

The Essex Coach

This ESSEX Six $945 *Freight and Tax Extra*

With Vibrationless Motor, Long Life and Balloon Tires

Why Hudson and Essex Outsell All Rivals

Still Another Reason
From The Wall Street Journal

Hudson Motor Car Co.'s recent statement that its sales of cars during the first seven and one-half months of 1924 were in excess of total business during the whole of 1923 calls attention to the exceptional position of this company, both as manufacturer and merchandiser. In view of the conditions which have beset nearly every producer during the past four months, this record of 95,000 cars in seven and one-half months this year against 88,000 cars in all of 1923 is entitled to more than ordinary notice.

Continuing personnel is another important factor in Hudson's remarkable showing. The same officials who "put Hudson over" when it was a small affair are still at the helm. There is a wealth of talent within the Hudson organization of which the public hears but little, which seems content to saw wood year in and year out, and to successfully evade the spotlight of personal publicity.

It is not merely because the Coach exclusively gives "Closed Car Comforts at Open Car Cost."

It is because both Hudson and Essex offer the most astounding value in genuine car PERFORMANCE and RELIABILITY.

It is because they have vibrationless motors—exclusive to them because they are built on the Super-Six principle.

More than 250,000 owners know their enduring value.

That is why they outsell all rivals—and why the Coach is the largest selling 6-cylinder closed car in the world.

An examination will convince you of quality not obtainable elsewhere within hundreds of dollars of these prices.

In Quality Hudson and Essex Are Alike

HUDSON Super-Six COACH $1395
Freight and Tax Extra

The Hudson engineers were pioneer designers and builders of low-priced closed cars, a type they named the "coach." Shown below is a 1923 Super Six Sedan, a closed car built along square lines. This model had manually controlled radiator shutters, drum headlights, a Boyce Motometer, and demountable rims. A permanent sun visor was attached to a sloping windshield and the upper portion of the windshield could be opened for ventilation.

At left is a reproduction of an ad for the low-priced Essex Coach, which offered "closed car comforts at open car cost." Hudson's Essex Coach at $945 was a remarkable value for a closed car in its day. The first Essex cars were powered with four-cylinder engines and the later models were of the six-cylinder type.

The great increase in Hudson's 1925 sales and profits was a result of their development of the low-priced Essex, the cost of which they cut from $1,000 in July, 1924, to $765 in 1926. Hudson sold over twice as many cars in 1925 (268,000) as they did in 1924 (133,000), and their profits almost tripled as a result of their endeavors in the low-priced field.

A Reputation for Speed

Directly below is the 1924 Essex Coach with the square, boxlike lines. At center is the 1928 Hudson Model "S" four-door Sedan. This car had four-wheel brakes and a very streamlined radiator ornament. The one-piece windshield was just coming in vogue.

Shown at bottom is the 1932 Hudson Straight Eight Standard Sedan, which proved to be an extremely fast and powerful car. Hudson has always had a reputation for exceptional acceleration, top speed, and power. Throughout the years, probably no one make of car has won more stock-car races than Hudson. Their automobiles were winning these races as early as 1909 and 1910, and they are still winning them today.

The International Harvester Company has long been a manufacturer of high-class farm equipment, trucks, and buses. In 1907 International entered the automobile field with a unique high-wheeled vehicle designed along buggy lines, which had solid rubber tires. Shown below is an International Auto Buggy powered by an air-cooled two-cylinder engine. The planetary transmission had two forward speeds, one reverse, and double chain drive was used. Under favorable conditions it could make 15 to 20 miles per hour. The rear seat could be removed, so that the car could be used as a light delivery wagon. This appealed to farmers and businessmen who could use the car as a light truck during the week, and on Sundays and evenings attach the rear seat for family outings. The bottom photograph shows the same model skillfully restored and in perfect working order today, a real collector's item.

Wagons and Buggies

Various models of the International, two of which are shown below, were sold through International dealers who usually handled farm equipment. These cars were the forerunners of the present International truck. They called the light truck an "Auto-Wagon," and the similar pleasure car an "Auto-Buggy."

The diagram directly below shows the layout of the 1908 Auto-Wagon and Auto-Buggy power plant. The automatic oiler was of the drip-feed type and the amount of oil flowing through the pipes to units requiring lubrication could be adjusted. Even the cooling-fan bearings that aided in cooling the cylinders were oiled automatically. The differential was on the jackshaft which was driven by a single chain, while final drive was by double chain to rear wheels. A magneto of original design was used. Priming cups on the top of each cylinder permitted the driver to insert a few drops of gasoline to aid in cold-weather starting. Toward the end of the high-wheel era, International Harvester Company also built a few thousand water-cooled automobiles.

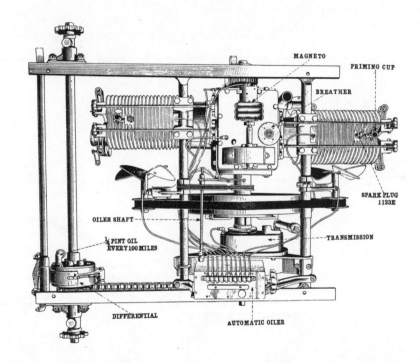

A Good Brake, 1907

The *International Owner's Book* of 1907 admitted that the brake was "one of the most important devices" on the automobile and claimed that the International auto had one of the best "*as long as the operator keeps it in adjustment.*" The early car owner had to know much more than we do today about what went on under the hood and elsewhere. The instructions as to how to keep the International brake in good working order were explicit and included a sketch (below). Another view of the 1907 model itself is pictured at bottom.

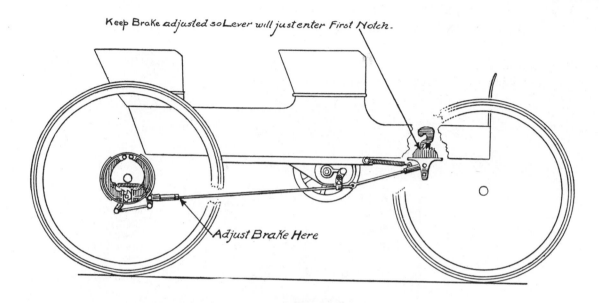

Keep Brake *adjusted so* Lever will just enter First Notch.

Adjust Brake Here

Two Cylinders and Air Cooling

Directly below is a typical International Auto-Wagon driver, sitting high above the road in his goggles and duster. Many drivers found this light truck to be suited to general use. At center, the same model as a single-seater with carrying capacity behind the seat. At bottom, an illustration of the air-cooled engine with overhead valves and "hairpin" instead of coil valve springs. A belt-driven fan aided in cooling each cylinder.

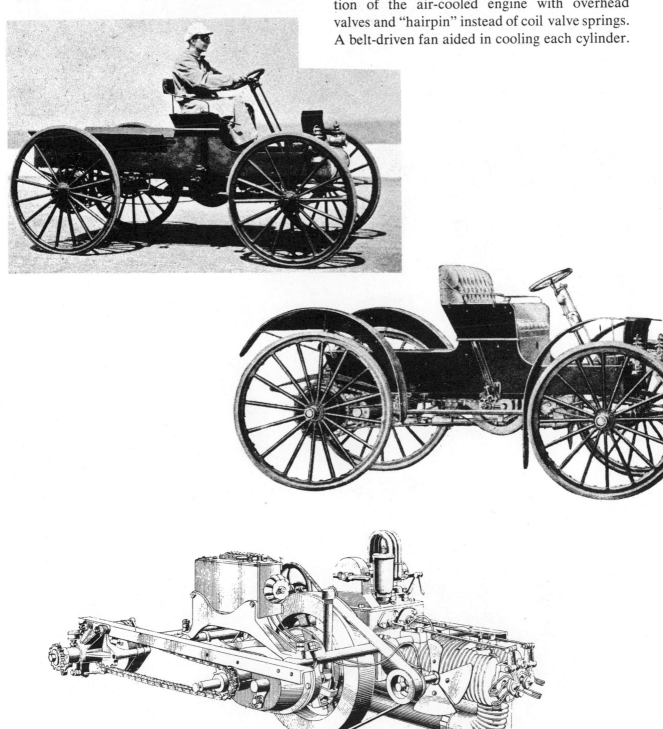

LINCOLN

Henry M. Leland, who was long connected with Cadillac as an engineer, started building his own Lincoln automobile in 1921. The car was similar to the Cadillac, but Mr. Leland introduced some engineering improvements. Even though the automobile was a superior one, production problems became quite serious for Mr. Leland and in 1922 he sold all of his interests in the Lincoln

Company to Henry Ford for a reported $12,-000,000. Starting in 1922, Lincolns were built by Ford, and many changes in style and design were effected. Leland, who had arranged in the transfer to remain with Ford, severed his connections after a few months, but the Ford Company continues its Lincoln efforts today.

Shown at the left is the 1922 Lincoln Sedan powered by the V-8 Leland-designed engine. This was a luxurious and dependable car. In the center, below, is the 1923 five-passenger Lincoln Coupé. Demountable rims and drum headlights were still retained, along with a sloping windshield and permanent visor. This car had automatic radiator shutters that were controlled by a thermostat. At bottom is the four-door, short-coupled sedan which was produced in 1924.

A Car with Class

Lincoln advertising was throughout the years consistently dignified and conservative, as evidenced by the 1926 Lincoln ad (below, left) for their two-passenger coupé. At right is a 1928 ad featuring the all-weather cabriolet. At bottom, left, is the four-passenger, 1932 Lincoln V-12 which they called the Sport Phaeton. At lower right is the V-12 LaBaron convertible four-passenger Sport Phaeton, which sold for $4,500 f.o.b Detroit. Twenty-one custom-built and standard body types were offered to V-12 Lincoln purchasers.

All-Weather Cabriolet

It has been so wisely said that minute attention to detail makes perfection. This truth is admirably illustrated in the Lincoln All-Weather Cabriolet. Even to the smallest detail this richly appointed car offers the very utmost in motoring satisfaction. Its interior fittings and appointments achieve a standard of comfort and convenience worthy of the satin-smooth performance of the precision-built Lincoln. The driver's compartment permits either Enclosed Drive or Town Car effect.

LINCOLN MOTOR COMPANY
Division of Ford Motor Company

NASH

When Charles W. Nash, former president of General Motors, purchased the Thomas B. Jeffery Company of Kenosha, Wisconsin, in 1916, he acquired the assets and good will of a company that was founded in 1879. In 1902 Jeffery had started building the Rambler car. Prior to that, Jeffery and his partner, R. Philip Gormley, had operated the profitable American Bicycle Company. The Jeffery car succeeded the Rambler, and the Nash succeeded the Jeffery. This firm, now owned by Nash Motors, has manufactured automobiles continuously for more than fifty years.

Shown at right is Thomas B. Jeffery himself in an experimental Rambler with the engine mounted on the side, built in 1901. Below, center, Mr. Jeffery is shown driving an experimental one-cylinder Rambler in a road test near Kenosha. Perhaps the wagon he is towing can be considered a forerunner of the trailer. The photograph at bottom shows how the assembly line looked when Rambler cars were being produced at the rate of 124 per month during 1902, the company's first year of operation.

The Early Ramblers

Directly below is the 1902 single-cylinder Rambler, Model C, which could be cranked from the seat. It had a large flywheel, a planetary transmission, full elliptical springs, and wire wheels on which were mounted single-tube tires. The price of this old buggy was $750. Above right is Dr. G. B. Christman of Fort Collins, Colorado, and his bride-to-be, in a 1902 Rambler Runabout.

At bottom, right, is an interesting 1903 Rambler ad from *Automobile Topics* magazine. The copy writer advised the reader that the single-cylinder auto had only half the number of parts and consequently only half the trouble of the two-cylinder car—perhaps an oversimplification, but still good selling technique. At bottom, left, is the two-cylinder Rambler Surrey with "rear entrance tonneau, canopy top, waterproof side curtains, and plate-glass swinging front windshield," to quote the catalogue. A wag once said that the single gas headlight jutting out in front also served as a bumper. This car had a planetary transmission, and luggage was carried in the wicker basket.

Rambler Power

In 1905, Rambler advertisements like the one below boasted of a chain transmission which applied every ounce of power the engine generated directly to the rear axle. The ad also featured the Rambler steering wheel, which controlled both the speed and direction of the car. The throttle was actually a round disc located directly beneath the steering wheel. The car illustrated in the ad could be purchased complete with lamps and tools for $1,200, but the cape top was $100 extra.

Below, right, is a 1908 four-cylinder Rambler with gas lights supplied by a carbide generator mounted in back of the front fender. Bumpers, top, windshield, and speedometer were all "extras." At lower left is the 1910 Rambler, a luxurious car with closed passenger compartment, which sold for $3,750. The chauffeur may have suffered from the dust and the breezes but at least he had a roof over his head.

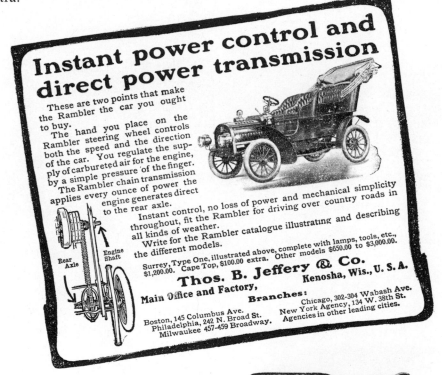

The Spare Wheel

The Rambler spare wheel, offered as early as 1909, was later called the "Fifth Wheel" and was supplied complete with inflated tire, but without hub center. By removing only six nuts, with special tools provided, a tire could be changed in three minutes. The Model Forty-four in the advertisement seated seven persons comfortably.

Model Forty-four, 34 H. P., $2,250
Spare Wheel, with Inflated Tire, Brackets, and Tools, $74. Magneto, $150

The Rambler Spare Wheel

Have you ever had to stop on the road to repair a punctured tire when you were in a hurry to reach your destination? All 1909 four-cylinder Ramblers are fitted for the Rambler Spare Wheel, a wheel complete, excepting hub center, with an inflated tire. Can be substituted for front or rear wheels within three minutes' time.   Only six nuts to remove—done quickly with special tools provided.

Completely obviates all tire worries; makes punctures mere incidents of a trip and saves the tiresome task of pumping up the new tire.   The price of the Rambler Spare Wheel complete is $74 or $85, according to tire size.

Write for catalog describing in detail Rambler offset crankshaft, straight-line drive, and other exclusive Rambler features.

Seven-passenger model, 45 horsepower, $2,500.   Other models, $1,150 to $2,500.

Thomas B. Jeffery & Company

Main Office and Factory, Kenosha, Wisconsin

Branches and Distributing Agencies

Chicago, Milwaukee, Cleveland, Boston, New York, San Francisco.   Representatives in all leading cities

THE CAR OF STEADY SERVICE

A Record, 1909

Rambler cars competed in many events, such as races and hill climbs, and Rambler drivers established a number of cross-country road records. Shown below is a 1909 Rambler ad telling of the record-breaking run from Los Angeles to San Diego, California—130 miles in 10 hours and 32 minutes. The four-cylinder Rambler beat the previous record, established by a six-cylinder car, by 45 minutes, and won the Chanslor-Lyon Challenge Cup. This Rambler was advertised as "the car of Steady Service." Notice the unusual winglike front fenders, which make the Rambler appear as though it were about ready to take off. The bucket seat at the rear was an extra, and the tires were smooth, without any tread design.

Rambler

Breaks Los Angeles - San Diego Record

New 32-H. P. Four-Cylinder Rambler Roadster Beats By 45 Minutes Time Record Established By Six-Cylinder Car And Is Awarded The Chanslor-Lyon Challenge Cup.

THREE hundred and thirty miles in ten hours and thirty-two minutes and not a single stop for repairs. That is the new round trip record between Los Angeles and San Diego, California, just established by the new 32 horse power, four-cylinder Rambler roadster.

This is the second time the Rambler has made this sensational run and each time it has broken all preceding records.

The first time the Rambler made the run in 11 hours and 31 minutes. Shortly afterwards a six-cylinder car reduced this time by a bare 14 minutes. The Rambler went after the record again, this time reducing its own time by nearly one hour.

There are certain mechanical features of the Rambler which make it possible for it to excel in consistent road performance any other car at any price. If you care to know what these features are, send us your address and we will be glad to send you our new catalog.

THE CAR OF STEADY SERVICE

Thomas B. Jeffery & Company, Main Office and Factory, Kenosha, Wis.

Branches and Distributing Agencies:

Chicago, Milwaukee, Boston, New York, Cleveland, San Francisco.   Representatives in all leading cities.

The "Cross-country" Model

The car (below) is the 1911 four-cylinder touring car with the celebrated fifth wheel. At bottom is the 1912 "Cross-country" model Rambler ($1,650). The passengers in this big touring car had just completed a 320-mile tour from Chicago to Toledo. The car performed so well that thereafter it was called the Cross-country model. After close inspection of the photograph, it is fair to assume that both car and occupants were considerably cleaned up after that 320-mile Chicago-Toledo run, for purposes of the camera and posterity.

Charles W. Nash

Charles W. Nash (left), one of the outstanding men in the automotive industry, came up the hard way. When he was six years old, he was "bound out" to a Michigan farmer for whom he was to work for room and board and no wages for fifteen years. Fortunately for himself and the industry, he ran away when he was twelve, and years later got a job in a wagon factory in Flint.

Below is the 1915 Jeffery Sedan with an unusual closed body, in that it has but a single door located at the extreme front. This model was the last of the cars to bear the Jeffery name. It was equipped with electric lights and demountable rims. At bottom is a 1918 Nash Touring Car with a six-cylinder overhead-valve engine. Nash took over the Jeffery Company in 1916, but this is actually the first Nash-designed car to be offered for sale.

Nash Trucks

During its long history, Nash has manufactured a few trucks, the most famous one being the Nash Quad. This car was a four-wheel-drive unit with ability to carry heavy loads under the worst possible conditions. Shown below is one of the many Nash Quads purchased by the United States government. Notice the mud chains on the front tires which were solid rubber. A single, centrally mounted gas headlight was used. At bottom is one of the early Nash Quads used by the Army, and standing alongside the car is General John J. "Black Jack" Pershing. This photo was taken along the Mexican border during the year 1916.

The Ajax Was a Nash

Like most successful motorcar manufacturers, Nash twice decided to produce cars bearing names other than his own. Many car-company officials felt that sales could be stimulated in different price brackets if the names were changed. Nash once manufactured the Lafayette V-8 car, designed by engineer D. McCall White, and in 1925 Nash brought out a low-priced car which he called the Ajax. Shown at the upper right, this two-door sedan had disc wheels with the

spare tire carried at the rear and the roof turned down slightly at the front. At left, top, is a 1923 Nash Sedan with steel disc wheels, drum headlights, and a single-piece windshield.

At bottom, right, is the 1926 Nash Advanced Six four-door Sedan. Bumpers were by this time considered standard equipment. At left center is shown a long and attractive 1930 Nash Cabriolet model with eight cylinders-in-line. This fast, powerful car had twin ignition. Wood wheels had replaced the formerly popular steel disc wheels.

Among his many notable contributions to the automobile world, Nash gave Walter Chrysler his first job in the business in 1911.

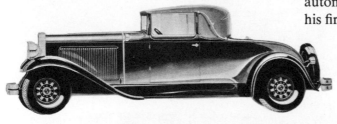

Oldsmobile

Automobile manufacturer Ransom E. Olds has the distinction of having built experimental cars powered by steam, electricity, and gasoline. The Olds Motor Vehicle Company was incorporated at Lansing, Michigan, on August 1, 1897. At right is a photo of an experimental Olds car. While the sign calls the car an "Oldsmobile," the name actually was not coined until a later date. Below it is a reproduction of the handwritten minutes of the directors' meeting held in 1897 at which "R. E. Olds was elected manager for the coming eleven months." In 1899 the Olds Motor Works was organized in Detroit, and 12 cars were built. In 1901, 386 cars were made, although production was delayed because of a fire in the Detroit factory. By 1902, Oldsmobiles were produced in Lansing and in the rebuilt Detroit factory, and production ran to 2,500 cars.

Gus Edwards wrote the famous song "In My Merry Oldsmobile" in 1905, and in that year 612 cars came from Oldsmobile factories. Shown below are illustrations from an Oldsmobile letterhead showing three separate Oldsmobile plants. At lower left is shown the Detroit plant which burned in 1901, but was rebuilt. This plant was later discontinued and the Olds activities were all moved to Lansing. At upper left is the Lan-

sing plant in 1902. At lower right is the Olds Gasoline Engine Works in Lansing, first started in 1885.

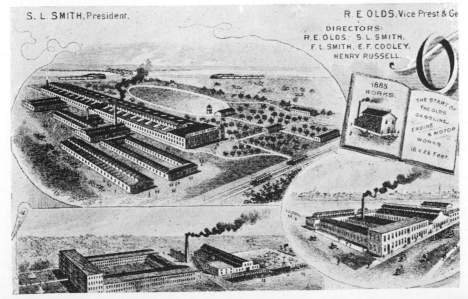

First Mass Production

The Olds gasoline engine was manufactured in the Lansing plant, shown directly below, from 1880 to 1885. This is the first shop of P. S. Olds (Ransom's father) and Son, and the engines were manufactured before Olds started to build automobiles. At right, below, is the second horseless carriage built by R. E. Olds in 1890. It was a steam car and was shipped to Bombay, India, in 1893. This vehicle with the fringe on the top ran 15 miles on the filling of water and 40 miles on the gasoline that fired the boiler. Shown at bottom is the engine assembly line taken at the Olds plant in 1901—surely one of America's first mass-production assembly lines.

Nature's Mistake

Ransom E. Olds hit the jackpot with his sleek curved-dash Oldsmobile. Shown at bottom, right, is the 1903 model, equipped with a single-cylinder engine located in the rear, and a planetary transmission. This car was probably the most famous of all the early automobiles made in the United States. For its day, it was a thoroughly reliable, economical and stylish automobile.

Early Olds ads like the one shown directly below pointed out with obvious bluntness that the curved-dash Oldsmobile was much better than the horse and buggy. The owner is trying to coax the horse into harness by offering it grain, while the owner of the Oldsmobile with his lady companion has already started upon his pleasure trip. At bottom, left, is a photograph of the disastrous fire at the Olds Motor Works' Detroit plant in the spring of 1901. The factory was later rebuilt.

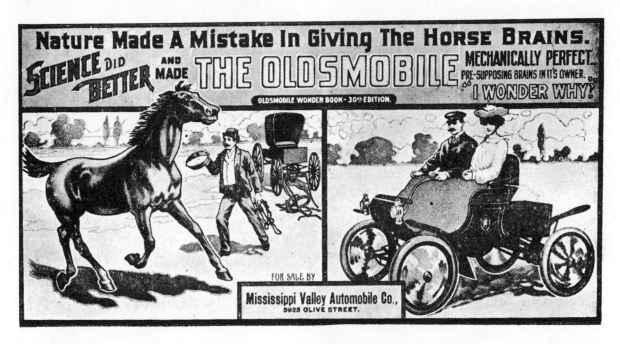

R. E. Olds

Ransom E. Olds (right), who died in 1950, will not soon be forgotten for his accomplishments in the automobile field. His activities in other areas, notably that of philanthropy, are perhaps less well known. In 1942, for instance, he established Olds Hall (Main Building shown directly below) in Daytona Beach, Florida, as a permanent home for retired ministers and missionaries. Also below is a sketch of the Olds Tower, built by its namesake, in Lansing. The 1902 ad at bottom describes the last Oldsmobile with wire wheels.

Price
$650,00
at Factory

Write Dept. P
for
Illustrated
Book

TWO of the nine Blue Ribbons (100 per cent.) for completing a strenuous 100 mile run without stop, at Chicago, August 2, 1902, were awarded

The Oldsmobile

The judges could not be shaken from their opinion that **The Oldsmobile is The Best Thing On Wheels,** for there is nothing to watch but the Road, and all roads are alike to the Oldsmobile, which is built to run *and does it.*

SELLING AGENTS

Oldsmobile Co., 138 W. 38th St., New York
Oldsmobile Co., 1124 Connecticut Ave., Washington
Quaker City Auto. Co., 138 N. Broad St., Philadelphia
H. B. Shattuck & Son, 239 Columbus Avenue, Boston
Banker Bros. Co., East End, Pittsburgh
Oldsmobile Company, 411 Euclid Ave., Cleveland, O.
William E. Metzger, 254 Jefferson Ave., Detroit
Ralph Temple & Austrian Co., 293 Wabash Ave., Chicago
Fisher Automobile Co., Indianapolis
Rochester Automobile Co., 170 South Av., Rochester, N. Y.

Olds Gasoline Engine Works, Omaha
W. C. Jaynes Auto. Co., 873 Main St., Buffalo, N. Y.
Day Automobile Co., St. Louis and Kansas City, Mo.
George Hannan, 1455 California Street, Denver
Clark & Hawkins, 903 Texas Ave, Houston, Texas
The Manufacturers Co,, 26 Fremont St. San Francisco
A. F. Chase & Co., 215 So. Third St., Minneapolis
Oldsmobile Co., 728 National Ave., Milwaukee, Wis.
Abbott Cycle Co., 411 Baronne St., New Orleans, La.
F. E. Gilbert, Jacksonville, Fla.

OLDS MOTOR WORKS, Detroit, Mich., U. S. A.

Olds's Development

The three cars directly below show some noteworthy phases of Olds's development. At top is a 1906 two-cylinder Oldsmobile with rear entrance tonneau. This model was produced when the curved-dash Olds's popularity was beginning to decline. In the center is the large six-cylinder Oldsmobile of 1909 with a spare tire in the back seat. At bottom is the 1923 six-cylinder Oldsmobile, still without bumpers.

Throughout the years, Oldsmobile has established many records for all kinds of competition.

In 1925 the author established a new stock car record at Pikes Peak in an Olds Six (see below). The total distance run was 12 miles; the total climb, 4,959 feet. Any car that makes that run in 28 minutes and 49 seconds even today is a rugged automobile.

Packard

In 1899 the first Packard was completed and driven under its own power in Warren, Ohio. Two brothers, William Dowd Packard (left) and James Ward Packard (right), formed a company that was to play an important part in automobile history. The first car, shown below, had a single-cylinder 12-horsepower engine. It was chain-driven and had a transmission with three forward speeds, quite extraordinary for 1899. The car had wire wheels with single tube tires and was steered by a tiller. The body was designed along buggy lines and had a patent-leather dashboard. Shown at bottom is the original Packard factory at Warren, Ohio.

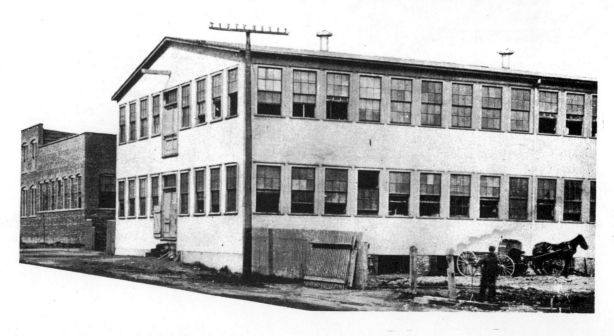

From Two to Four Cylinders

One of the first Packard cars was sold to Henry B. Joy, who liked it so much that he decided to finance the development of the car. By 1904 he was producing the Packard car himself, as James Ward Packard was no longer connected with the company. Apparently Packard lacked faith in the future of the automobile—although he had early shown his inventive genius in the field—and went back to manufacturing cables in Warren, Ohio. Directly below is a 1902 Packard Runabout. At right is a 1905 Packard ad for the Model N that appeared in *Automobile Topics* magazine. This car, at $3,500, was one of the luxury cars then being manufactured.

At bottom, right, is the original inventor, James Ward Packard, in his 1904 model. The rear seat could be quickly detached and it appears as though its installation may have been decided upon after the car was built.

The new Model N Packard combines all the proven excellence of our Model L, with the addition of more power, longer wheel base and double side entrance body.

The car will take all reasonable hills on the high gear and yet easily maintain 45 miles per hour over ordinary country roads.

Every available ounce of power developed by the 4-cylinder motor is nursed upon ball bearings, and is transmitted upon the high speed through a bevel gear direct drive.

The lubrication of the motor is positive, being accomplished by a gear driven single plunger pump. The carburetor automatically adjusts itself to every variation of motor speed and is not affected by atmospheric changes.

The perfect control of the motor without removing the hands from the steering wheel, the noiselessness of the transmission, both in shifting and in operation, the smooth action of the clutch and the faultless ignition system are all exclusive PACKARD features.

Wheel base 106 inches, rear springs 50 inches, all tires 34x4, tonneau extra roomy—will comfortably seat three large people.

Price (with standard Equipment) $3,500.00, f. o. b. Detroit

For our new catalogue and name of the nearest Packard dealer, address

Packard Motor Car Co., Dept. B, Detroit, Mich.

Member A. L. A. M.

NEW YORK BRANCH
1840 BROADWAY

Three Early Packards

The Packard Company was among the first to offer significant improvements in the automobile field. The top photograph below is of the 1906 Packard. In this year magneto ignition was introduced, and production reached an all-time high of 700 cars. The stationary windshield and side curtains offered protection to the driver of this aristocratic automobile. No bumper was used, and gas headlights were considered accessories, although the brackets to hold the headlights can be seen in front of the radiator.

The 1909 Packard Roadster (below, center) with an extra single seat in the rear was truly a sporting car. Precision workmanship had by then given Packard an international reputation. Note how the fenders taper smartly to a small step for entering.

At bottom is the 1911 Touring Car with right-hand drive and four doors for the comfort of driver and passengers. The early Packard formula—sell 1,000 cars and make $1,000,000 —was particularly effective between 1905 and 1910. It was easier to sell expensive cars to wealthy people than it was to sell medium-priced cars to middle-class people.

The Famous "Twin Six"

The elaborate 1915 Packard "Twin Six" Coupé is shown directly below. The "Twin Six" created a sensation in automobile circles by the smooth and flexible operation of its engine. The car had distinctive headlights, a folding windshield, and two spare tires could be carried.

The center photograph shows the 1916 seven-passenger sedan. This two-tone luxury car was one of the roomiest sedans offered by any manufacturer. Note the homelike window shades in the back seat and the eight windows. At bottom is the 1919 popular-model small coupé.

PLYMOUTH

The first Chrysler-produced Plymouth (directly below) was introduced the year the Republican Party nominated and elected Herbert Hoover President of the United States and the year before the bottom dropped out of the stock market. It had hydraulic brakes, Floating Power, and a high-compression engine. At left is a Plymouth bus manufactured by the Commercial Motor Truck Company of Plymouth, Ohio, in 1908. Walter Chrysler had no connection with this company which manufactured automobiles, buses, and gasoline-powered railroad cars. Below, left, a 1928 four-door Plymouth, and below, right, the 1929 Plymouth four-door Sedan.

Four Plymouths, 1930–1933

Nineteen-thirty was a year of memorable news events. Admiral Byrd returned from his Antarctic explorations. The ocean liner *Europa* set a new transatlantic record, Mahatma Gandhi was once again arrested in India. Here at home, the economic depression cut automobile sales severely except in the case of the newly born Plymouth, whose dealers in 1930 doubled their 1929 sales. In 1931, Lou Miller made auto news by driving a Chrysler from San Francisco to New York in 132 hours and 9 minutes, setting a new transcontinental record.

Top, right, is the 1930 four-door sedan which sold for $695. A 1931 sedan is shown below, left. In 1932 Plymouth sales reached 111,-926 and the Chrysler Corporation introduced the new Plymouth Six (bottom, left). By 1933, only five years after the car was first produced, Plymouth had grown in public favor to the extent that approximately one out of every four low-priced cars sold was a Plymouth. The 1933 four-door sedan is pictured at bottom right.

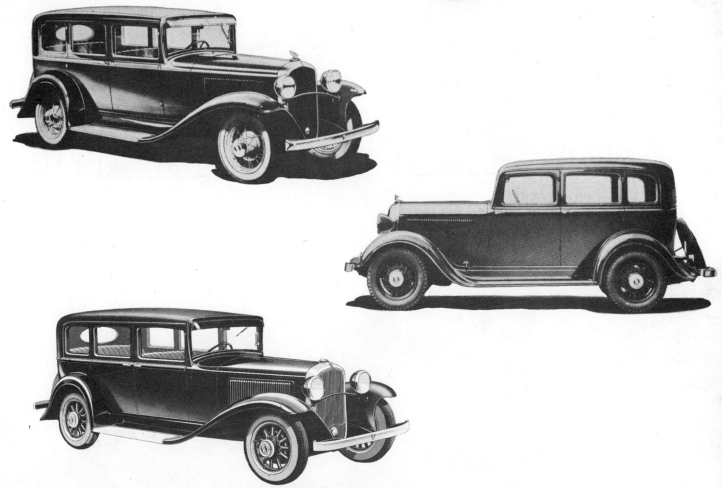

PONTIAC

The first Pontiac, advertised below, was not manufactured by General Motors, but was a product of the Pontiac Motor Vehicle Company of Pontiac, Michigan. This 1908 ad gives details of this early high-wheeler.

The illustration at left shows the first factory of the Oakland Motor Car Company, also in Pontiac, Michigan. The Oakland, designed by A. P. Brush, was the forerunner of today's Pontiac. At bottom is the 1909 Oakland Touring Sedan. This was the year William C. Durant purchased the car for General Motors. This car had four cylinders, full elliptic rear springs, gas headlights, and a bulb horn. The engine ran in a counterclockwise direction, similar to that of the single-cylinder Brush, also designed by A. P. Brush.

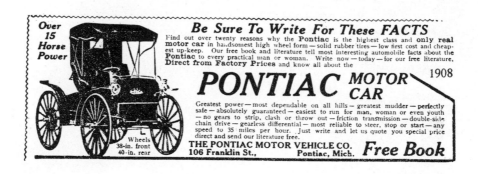

Chief of the Sixes

The early Oakland ad at right describes the merits of the 40-horsepower touring car which sold at $1,700 in 1910. By 1912, General Motors was producing the Oakland, the Buick, the Cadillac, and the Oldsmobile.

Directly below is the 1918 Oakland Roadster. This six-cylinder car had snappy styling and was equipped with demountable rims. Bumpers were extra.

In the center, at right, is the 1924 Oakland, the first make of automobile to be finished in Du Pont Duco, which reduced by days the time required to paint an automobile.

At bottom, right, is the 1926 Pontiac Coach, built when the coach, a low-priced two-door sedan, was very popular. This was the first Pontiac built by General Motors and was the direct successor to the Oakland, which was discontinued at this time. At bottom, left, is a 1927 Pontiac Landau Sedan. The Pontiac more than exceeded in popularity even General Motors's expectations. In the first year of Pontiac production, G.M. had to appropriate an extra $5,000,-000 so that Pontiac capacity could meet the demand.

The Undefeated Oakland

"40" H. P. Touring Car $1,700

The Oakland "40" in power, dimensions, appearance and performance is in the class with any of the three thousand dollar cars.

As a hill climber the Oakland is entirely in a class by itself. The "40" has won first place in its class in every event it started during the season, including the following:

Fort George Hill, New York City
Giants' Despair, Wilkesbarre, Pa.
Morgan Hill, Logansport, Ind.

Newport Hill, Cleveland
Algonquin Hill, Chicago
Hoopestown Hill, Ill.

It has won the free-for-all hill climbing contests at Fort Ancient Hill, Cincinnati, and Columbus Avenue, Mount Vernon, N. Y., defeating many cars selling for two or three times its price, including a number of Four Thousand and Five Thousand Dollar Cars.

All models have three-speed sliding gear, selective type transmission, and include magneto and full lamp equipment, and are high grade in every detail.

Oakland "30" H. P. Touring Car $1,250
Oakland "30" H. P. Runabout $1,000

Shepherd Motor Car Co., 1785 Broadway
Made by OAKLAND MOTOR CAR CO.   PONTIAC, MICH.

REO

Ransom E. Olds had a difference of opinion with Frederick Smith of Oldsmobile about the size and price of their car. Olds wanted to continue making the inexpensive, dependable automobile, priced at $695, and Smith wanted to make large, higher-priced cars. Late in 1903, Olds left the Oldsmobile Company and from the experience gained in building the single-cylinder Oldsmobile, he started production of his new car, the Reo, with wheel steering, in 1904. Two models were manufactured. The single-cylinder runabout had a folding rear seat that could be detached. The single-cylinder Reo shown at left had a hood which housed the water and gasoline tanks and the radiator. Full elliptic springs and battery ignition were standard equipment.

Below are two other photos of early Reos. The passenger holding his hat (directly below) is Mr. Olds himself. At the bottom, the man on the sidewalk with a package under his arm may be Mr. Olds.

T.R. in a Reo

When he left Oldsmobile and started another company, Olds obviously could not use his name to identify the new car. Instead he lent his initials, R.E.O., to the new venture. His reputation was so great in the early days that if a car could be identified with his genius and his record, it would have a definite advantage over competitive makes. Many colorful stunts were organized to promote the sale of Reo cars, one of which is shown in the illustration below. The company used to have its own band which staged Saturday parades and concerts to popularize the car.

At right is a photograph of one of Theodore Roosevelt's first public rides in an automobile. This 1908 two-cylinder, five-passenger Reo Touring Car is being driven by Ransom E. Olds himself, the only man in the car wearing a derby.

Always Up-to-Date

By R. E. Olds, Designer

In Reo the Fifth, new ideas are adopted as soon as the leaders accept them. The car is kept up-to-date.

Thus, at any time this car contains about every new feature in sight.

And most of the time one finds the car months in advance of its rivals.

Reo the Fifth Roadster

Next Year's Cars

The evidence is that most next year's cars will adopt the following features. The leading cars already have them.

Note that Reo the Fifth, as we build it today, embodies all these coming features.

Left-side drive
Center control
Electric lights
Set-in dash lights
Oversize tires

There is no need to argue these. Note the leaders of Motordom—how all of them have them. There is no better evidence that cars without them will soon be obsolete.

One-Rod Control

Another feature bound to come is the Reo one-rod control.

Note what it means. No levers in the driver's way, either side or center. The driver's entrance on either side is absolutely clear. He never dismounts in the street.

All the gear shifting is done by one small center rod. It is done by moving this rod only three inches in each of four directions. Both brakes are operated by foot pedals.

No coming feature means as much to the driver as this simple rod control, this absence of levers, this clear entrance in front.

Things That Still Must Come

There are other features in Reo the Fifth to which cars of this class must come.

Men expect them in costly cars. But men are bound to demand them in any car when they know what their absence

means. I refer to things like these:

Analyzed steel
Properly tested gears
15 roller bearings
190 drop forgings
High-test magneto
Doubly-heated carburetor
Vast overcapacity
Utter exactness
Slow, careful building
Insurance against flaws

I have spent 26 years building automobiles. I know their short-comings—know what cars must stand.

Time will force all makers, as it forced me, into these extreme precautions.

Steel must be made to formula—must be analyzed twice—to be sure of the needed strength. Gears must be tested in a crushing machine, not with a hammer.

Timken bearings cost five times as much as common ball bearings. But they must be used, and used everywhere—not only in the largest bearings.

Drop forgings are costly, but steel castings too often have flaws. Strength that seems sufficient often proves insufficient. Big margins of safety are needed. In Reo the Fifth, every driving part is given 50 per cent overcapacity. Parts should be hand-fitted and ground over and over. Every part should be given a radical test. Engines, after testing, should be taken apart and inspected.

We Do All This

In Reo the Fifth all these things are done. They are costly, but we save their cost by building only one

model, by making all our parts, by modern machinery, by extreme efficiency.

Our price proves that such things need not be expensive—need not be confined to the high-cost cars.

As a result, each Reo the Fifth is an utterly perfect car. It is almost a trouble-proof car. The extra cost to us is saved over and over in your up-keep cost. And year after year this car keeps running as well as it runs when new.

More and more, the men who know demand this class of car. Our sales this year have broken all our records.

———

A thousand dealers sell Reo the Fifth. If you don't know the nearest, write or telegraph for address.

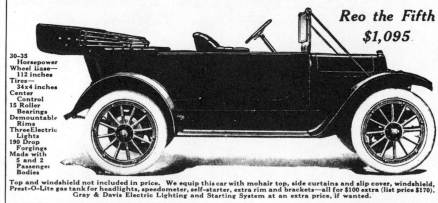

Reo the Fifth $1,095

30-35 Horsepower
Wheel Base— 112 inches
Tires— 34x4 inches
Center Control
15 Roller Bearings
Demountable Rims
Three Electric Lights
190 Drop Forgings
Made with 5 and 2 Passenger Bodies

Top and windshield not included in price. We equip this car with mohair top, side curtains and slip cover, windshield, Prest-O-Lite gas tank for headlights, speedometer, self-starter, extra rim and brackets—all for $100 extra (list price $170). Gray & Davis Electric Lighting and Starting System at an extra price, if wanted.

R. M. Owen & Co. General Sales Agents for Reo Motor Car Co., Lansing, Mich.

Canadian Factory, St. Catharines, Ont.

(206)

REO

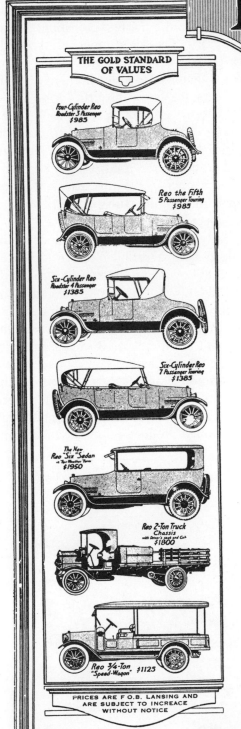

THE GOLD STANDARD
OF VALUES

Four-Cylinder Reo
Roadster 3 Passenger
$985

Reo the Fifth
5 Passenger Touring
$985

Six-Cylinder Reo
Roadster 4 Passenger
$1385

Six-Cylinder Reo
7 Passenger Touring
$1385

The New
Reo "Six" Sedan
at Two-Weather Town
$1950

Reo 2-Ton Truck
Chassis
with Driver's seat and Cab
$1800

Reo ¾-Ton
"Speed-Wagon" $1125

PRICES ARE F.O.B. LANSING AND
ARE SUBJECT TO INCREACE
WITHOUT NOTICE

Every Reo Dealer
is Oversold

THAT'S THE REMARKABLE thing about Reo demand. It is not only an all season's demand, but it is also an all State's demand.

IT IS UNIFORM—Reos are as popular in the South as in the North—on the Pacific as on the Atlantic Coast.

THEREIN REOS DIFFER from most makes of cars.

IN ONE CITY or State you will find a certain make of car very popular—in the next city they'll tell you they "never heard of" that car.

IF THE DEMAND happens, at times, to be **excessive** in a certain territory, the factory can switch a few shipments from another to help out.

NOT SO WITH REOS. Every one of the two thousand Reo Dealers is calling for more—calling all the time, too.

THERE ARE NO BARE SPOTS in Reo demand—no luke-warm territory.

AND THAT'S BECAUSE buyers are about the same everywhere. They are all looking for a product of sterling worth— reasonable first cost, low up-keep.

AND THROUGHOUT THE LAND Reo automobiles and motor trucks are known and accepted as "The Gold Standard of Values."

REO MOTOR CAR COMPANY
LANSING MICHIGAN

In 1904 (see below) some lucky girl was given the title "Miss Reo." It appears that one Stanley L. Emery, an aggressive salesman, conceived the idea to commemorate the first car shipped from the Reo factory. The 1904 model is shown in front of a 1926 Reo car with the "Miss Reo" of 1926. It is difficult to say which changed more in twenty years, the car or the girl.

By 1929 Reo was making a name for itself as the builder of exceptionally good trucks. The Reo "Speed Wagon" became one of the first high-speed trucks to be used on United States highways, as shown by the advertisement at left which appeared in the June, 1929, issue of *Successful Farming* magazine.

In the early thirties, the depression dealt the automobile industry a terrible blow. In 1932 Reo produced 3,800 cars and the next year only 3,600. In 1934, Olds, whose position had become chiefly honorary, resumed active control and direction of the company but his reentry on the scene made little difference. Reo was not producing as many cars as its founder had turned out for Oldsmobile in 1901. Fortunately, the Reo Company was one of those which managed to weather the bleak days of the thirties, although they discontinued production of passenger cars.

Studebaker

In 1852, more than a century ago, Henry and Clem Studebaker opened a blacksmith and wagon shop (right) at South Bend, Indiana. In 1857 the United States government ordered 100 wagons from them for the Army and that same year the Studebaker brothers built their first buggy. In 1864, Peter Studebaker joined his brothers as sales manager, and a fourth brother, Jacob, joined the firm in 1868. A sketch of the 1868 Studebaker plant is shown below. Thus, for more than 100 years Studebaker has manufactured quality vehicles of various types and designs.

At bottom is the death notice of Clement Studebaker, first president of the company, who served from 1868 until his death on November 27, 1901.

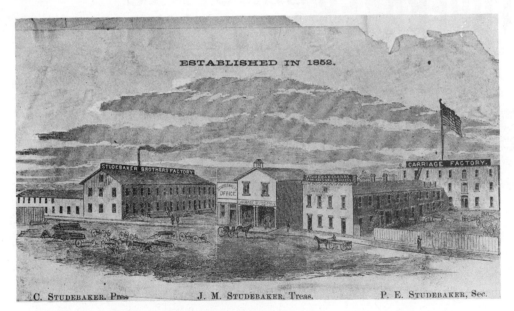

ESTABLISHED IN 1852.

C. STUDEBAKER, Pres   J. M. STUDEBAKER, Treas.   P. E. STUDEBAKER, Sec.

In Loving Remembrance
of a
Devoted Husband, a Tender Father,
a Helpful Friend and a
Useful Citizen
this notice is given of the death of
Clement Studebaker,
Wednesday, November 27, 1901,
Aged 70 years, 8 months and 15 days.
"Blessed are the Dead Which Die in the Lord"
Mrs. Clement Studebaker and Family,
Tippecanoe Place,
South Bend, Indiana

"No Expert Chauffeur Needed"

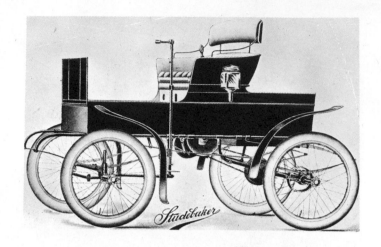

As early as 1902 the Studebaker brothers had the vision to foresee the beginning of the end for horse-drawn vehicles. They then decided to enter the horseless-carriage business. Their first car was a stylish light electric runabout (shown at left), built along buggy lines and first manufactured in 1902. It had leather fenders, bar-lever steering, chain drive, and a leather dashboard. The advertisement for this car (below) claims "Reliable Brake Control . . . All Machines Equipped with Two Brakes."

At bottom is the first Studebaker gasoline-powered car, built in 1904. Its two-cylinder engine developed 16 horsepower, and the wheelbase was 82 inches. Price, $1,600.

Gas and Electric

By 1906 Studebaker was offering the four-cylinder gasoline model shown below. It had 28 horsepower, 104-inch wheelbase, 34 x 4 tires, and the price was $3,000. The car seated five, had a gasoline capacity of 14 gallons, and came in four colors.

At right is one of the first closed horseless carriages manufactured in the United States. This electric coupé was manufactured by Studebaker in 1906–1907. It sold for $2,200 and would do about 35 miles on one charging of the batteries. Note the wooden wheels, chain drive, and running boards instead of steps. Studebaker's craftsmanship in carriage building stood them in good stead when this unusual vehicle was designed. It was considered, and rightfully so, one of the true quality automobiles of its time.

At right, below, is an interesting advertisement singing the praises of the 1910 Studebaker "40." Even this early, a Studebaker car is shown beside a team of oxen on a tour through the chateau district of France. The total car-cost of this tour through France, Spain, and Italy was claimed to have been only $3.80. Is that $3.80 a day?

TOURING IN A STUDEBAKER THROUGH THE CHATEAU DISTRICT OF FRANCE

Suitability of the car for constant family use and touring is the principal feature of the *Studebaker*.

It is essentially a three hundred and sixty-five days in the year automobile for general utility. Each individual part harmonizes thoroughly with reference to the service the car is intended to perform. It affords the maximum of

COMFORT, STYLE and DEPENDABILITY

Send for a well-known motorist's diary of a recent tour of France, Spain and Italy, made in a *Studebaker* at a total car-cost of $3.80. Fascinating as a story, replete with valuable touring information and data, and convincing as proof of *Studebaker* dependability.

Address Dept. D

STUDEBAKER AUTOMOBILE CO., General Offices: SOUTH BEND, IND.

Branches and Agencies Everywhere

7 Passenger
40 H. P.

Only American
car with Bosch
Low Tension
Magnetic Plugs

LICENSED UNDER SELDEN PATENT

Studebaker-Garford "40"

The 1910–1911 Studebaker "40" was actually a Garford car made in Elyria, Ohio. Studebaker became sales representatives for the car, previously called the Studebaker-Garford.

South Bend Factory, 1912

The 1911 Studebaker Limousine shown below had 40 horsepower, 117-inch wheelbase, and carried a list price of $4,500. It was built for the carriage trade, with a speaking tube over the right ear of the chauffeur for receiving instructons.

Below is the massive Studebaker plant at South Bend, Indiana, in 1912. The company at that time still manufactured wagons and carriages as well as operating the Studebaker Harness Company which produced harness and saddlery.

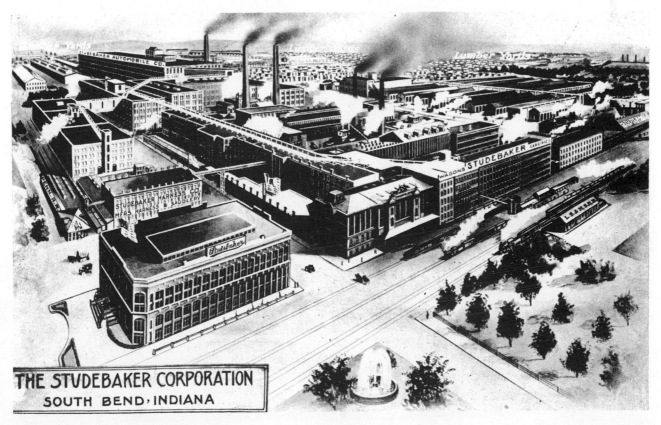

Light Six and Big Six

The Studebaker E-M-F "30" (top photo) was an attractive 1912 model priced at $1,190. It had four doors, a bulb horn, and the generator on the running board furnished gas for the headlights.

The second photo below shows a 1913 seven-passenger Tourer with a 27.2-horsepower engine and a list price of $1,290. This car was fast, powerful, and had folding auxiliary seats in the rear. The windshield folded down at the center as shown, and a toolbox was on the running board.

The third photo below is of a 1921 Studebaker Light Six Landau. This two-passenger roadster had a wheelbase of 112 inches and its list price was $1,650. It developed 23.4 horsepower. The 1922 Big Six Studebaker Speedster (shown at bottom) was listed at $1,985. It was exceptionally fast for its time.

The Erskine

Shown in the top photo, below, is a 1925 Standard Six Brougham Studebaker. Horsepower was 27.3, wheelbase 113 inches. The price was $1,465 for this fancy model with the "porthole" rear windows.

Like many another American manufacturer, Studebaker had a fling at building a lower-priced car carrying a name other than that of its regular line. The Erskine Six was named for A. R. Erskine, Studebaker president from 1915 to 1933.

Shown at bottom is the 1927 Erskine Six-cylinder Custom Coupé Model 50. This car was sold at the exceptionally low price of $985. Folding auxiliary rear seats ("rumble seats," as they became known) were popular in 1927.

Studebaker in Competition

The 1928 Studebaker President Eight shown in the top photo was driven 30,000 miles on the Atlantic City Speedway to establish a new American stock-car record in 1928.

Another low-priced car Studebaker manufactured in 1932 was named after Notre Dame's great football coach, Knute Rockne. (Studebaker's home, South Bend, Indiana, is also Notre Dame's.) The model shown below, center, is the Rockne Six Coupé. It had 66 horsepower, 110-inch wheelbase, and its price was $620 f.o.b. South Bend.

At bottom is Driver Cliff Bergere and the Studebaker he drove to third place in the 1932 Indianapolis 500-mile race. His mechanic is Vern Lake. Other Studebakers finished sixth, thirteenth, fifteenth, and sixteenth. This Studebaker performance at Indianapolis has excelled that of any other make of car using stock production engines.

White

The White Company, pioneer builder of sewing machines and prominent manufacturers of trucks today, decided to enter the automobile business in 1900. Below is the factory in which the first White steam cars were manufactured, on Canal Street in Cleveland, Ohio.

The first White steam car ever to be made, the Stanhope, is pictured at right. This car had a flash generator instead of the then conventional tubular boiler. The water entered at the top of the coil and was converted into steam before it reached the bottom. The car was invented by Rollin H. White and is now on display in the Smithsonian Institution, Washington, D.C.

The two trucks pictured at bottom were used in 1906 by the White Sewing Machine Company. The steering wheel was vertically mounted and solid tires were used.

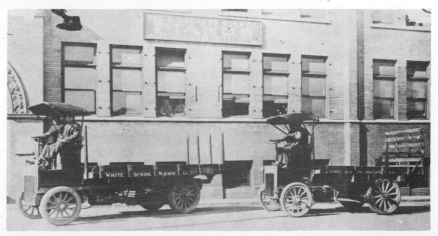

Walter White at the Wheel

One of the earliest White steam racing cars is pictured directly below. The driver is Walter White, who established many speed records during his early days as a race driver. Notice the many lugs between the spokes, necessary to hold the tire to the rim.

At the right is a 1906 White Steamer with President William Howard Taft seated at left rear. White Steamers were used as official White House cars and for other government uses before 1908.

The middle photograph below shows a White Steamer which competed in the celebrated Glidden Tour through Canada in 1906.

The photo at bottom was taken in 1909 to show seven years of White progress, starting with a 1902 model at the extreme left. All these cars are steamers, and their steady progression in size, from a very small to a very large car, is startling.

White Gasoline Car, 1910

The White gasoline car shown here is the model manufactured in 1910 and 1911. For a short time, the White Company manufactured both steam and gasoline cars. When steam-car popularity was on the decline, White had the foresight to get into the manufacturing of quality gasoline cars, and for several years one of the best passenger automobiles manufactured in the United States was the White. It had a four-speed transmission, magneto ignition, and other features that usually were offered only in the higher-priced cars. The body was of aluminum instead of sheet iron or "some other cheap substitute," as mentioned by White in this advertisement.

White advertising always stressed its product's high quality. While White passenger cars are no longer manufactured, the company has survived and throughout the years has built high-quality trucks and buses that are sold all over the world.

The first White truck, a steamer, was built and sold in 1900 to the Denver Dry Goods Company. When it proved to be a success, the Denver firm ordered another, and White—one-time builder of sewing machines and a number of other products—was launched in a new field, which grew so rapidly that a new company had to be established. By 1911, the White Company had eight branch offices.

Cars and Trucks

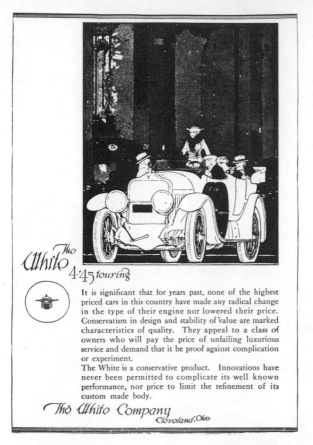

The White 4-45 touring

It is significant that for years past, none of the highest priced cars in this country have made any radical change in the type of their engine nor lowered their price. Conservatism in design and stability of value are marked characteristics of quality. They appeal to a class of owners who will pay the price of unfailing luxurious service and demand that it be proof against complication or experiment.

The White is a conservative product. Innovations have never been permitted to complicate its well known performance, nor price to limit the refinement of its custom made body.

The White Company
Cleveland, Ohio

Early auto advertisements rarely hesitated to call a spade a spade. The 1915 White ad about "Imitations" (below) does not balk at telling the facts, at least as the White Company saw them. Other cars might be imitations, but "leadership cannot be duplicated."

At upper left is a conservative advertisement about a superior product, the 1916 White 4-45 Touring Car. Below it is a 1916 White truck ad. This heavy-duty truck is so large and sits so high off the ground that it almost dwarfs the ship in the background.

"IMITATIONS"

YOU are in the theatre. At some moment during the performance some one kindly steps from the wings and delivers "a few imitations."

These "imitations" are clever—but imitations have their limitations.

They rest upon a twist of the mouth, a lift of an eyebrow, a hunch of the shoulder, an emphasized accent.

You applaud them—sometimes—but you would applaud the ORIGINAL a hundred times more.

❖ ❖ ❖

Leadership cannot be duplicated. It is always emphasized by imitation. Imitations are necessarily superficial—seldom as much as skin deep.

The history of White Motor Cars is one of origination, proving, introduction—and being imitated.

Months ago the latest White cars, with their finally-perfect streamline bodies, with the center cowl absorbing the conventional back of the front seat, offered inspirations for imitations.

The features which you SEE are being imitated, just as the stage imitator copies one or two prominent characteristics of the star whose leadership is so firmly established that an imitation is recognized.

It is one proposition to buy something because it looks a little bit like another.

But every standpoint of value comes into consideration when you select that which has established the principles which invite imitation.

The White body, IN ITS COMPLETENESS, makes made-to-order automobile bodies unnecessary for even the most critical taste.

Within that body, however, is the MECHANICAL completeness, which justifies the external beauty.

And there, after all, is the true standard of value. Looks, without SERVICE, would be an imitation of what you want.

❖ ❖ ❖

Leadership must and does create value.

Imitation need create nothing. It needs but wait.

The selection and purchase of a White Motor Car signifies that you secure the tangible value involved in long years of experience, the best engineering ability, and a consistent manufacturing policy.

And that you own and drive the acknowledged leader—the car which sets motor car fashion for America.

All White dealers are showing and demonstrating the latest White cars.

THE WHITE COMPANY, Cleveland
Manufacturers of Gasoline Motor Cars, Motor Trucks and Taxicabs
Exhibiting at Transportation Building, Panama-Pacific International Exposition, San Francisco

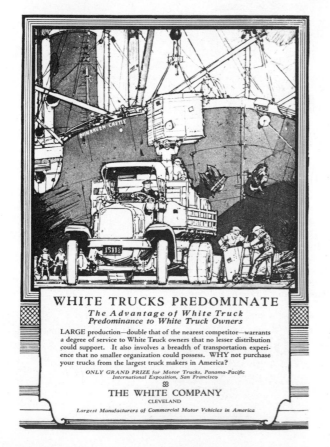

WHITE TRUCKS PREDOMINATE
The Advantage of White Truck Predominance to White Truck Owners

LARGE production—double that of the nearest competitor—warrants a degree of service to White Truck owners that no lesser distribution could support. It also involves a breadth of transportation experience that no smaller organization could possess. WHY not purchase your trucks from the largest truck makers in America?

ONLY GRAND PRIZE for Motor Trucks, Panama-Pacific International Exposition, San Francisco

THE WHITE COMPANY
CLEVELAND

Largest Manufacturers of Commercial Motor Vehicles in America

Willys

John N. Willys, an energetic salesman from Elmira, New York, who set the automotive world afire selling Overland products, became disgusted when he could not secure automobiles fast enough from the Indianapolis factory in 1907. He rushed to Indianapolis, only to find that the company did not have enough capital on hand to meet its payroll. Mr. Willys advanced $500 toward the payroll and then took over the company. Under his direction, the company prospered almost immediately. Years later, in 1923, Willys brought Walter Chrysler into the business as vice-president.

At right is a 1909 Overland ad. By 1911 the Willys-Overland Company had moved to Toledo, Ohio, where it has been one of the principal industries of that city ever since. Directly below is the first Overland car, manufactured in 1905. This vehicle had tiller steering, was cranked in front, and had a sloping hood and radiator.

The 1909 Willys-Overland test car at bottom, right, is driven by Percy Grubbs, Indianapolis sales manager, with Ernest Ethington, a tester, his passenger. It was powered by a four-cylinder engine with three-point suspension support. It had a planetary two-speed transmission, and a double ignition system with high-tension magneto and batteries.

The *Overland*

Model 30 - - - - - $1250
With Double Bucket Seats in rear - $1300

4 cylinder   30 H. P.
108" Wheel Base   32 x 3½ Q. D. Tires
         Magneto and Headlights

Unquestionably the best value ever placed
on the American market

Write for Catalog to
Overland Automobile Co.
Indianapolis :: :: :: Indiana

Plant Efficiency

This 1911 advertisement shows a bird's-eye view of the Willys-Overland factory at Toledo, said to be the largest and most thoroughly modern factory of its kind in the world. The company in 1911 was not too shy when it came to making statements about Overland superiority. But their claims must have been based on solid fact, for the firm has weathered many an economic storm throughout the years. Today it enjoys a world-wide reputation as the manufacturer of quality products, having produced hundreds of thousands of vehicles such as the two- and four-wheel-drive jeeps, station wagons, and commercial vehicles. In addition, the company now manufactures a thoroughly modern, dependable car in the low-priced field.

All this success rests in great part on the daring activities of John North Willys who, during the 1907 recession, took over the failing Overland Company and its $80,000 debt and breathed new life into it. In 1908 Willys-Overland came back from the grave to produce 465 cars. By 1909, after his move to Toledo, Willys made 4,000 cars and—incredibly—the company manufactured 18,200 automobiles in 1910. Willys' early exploits are fully as amazing as those of the genius behind General Motors, William Crapo Durant.

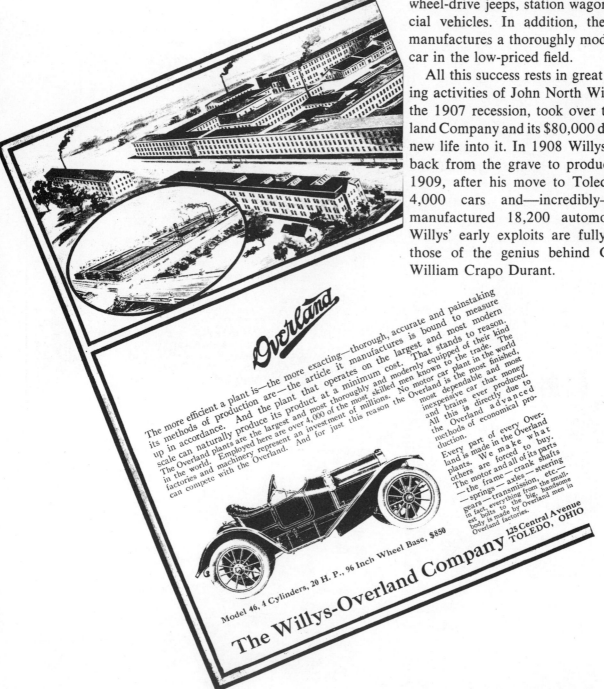

Overland

The more efficient a plant is—the more exacting—thorough, accurate and painstaking its methods of production are—the article it manufactures is bound to measure up in accordance. And the plant that operates on the largest and most modern scale can naturally produce its product at a minimum cost. That stands to reason. The Overland plants are the largest and most thoroughly and modernly equipped of their kind in the world. Employed here are over 4,000 of the most skilled men known to the trade. The factories and machinery represent an investment of millions. No motor car plant in the world can compete with the Overland. And for just this reason the Overland is the most finished, most dependable and most inexpensive car that money and brains ever produced.

All this is directly due to the Overland advanced methods of economical production.

Every part of every Overland is made in the Overland plants. We make what others are forced to buy. The motor and all of its parts —the frame—crank shafts —springs—axles—steering gears—transmission, etc.—in fact, everything from the smallest bolts to the big, handsome body is made by Overland men in Overland factories.

Model 46, 4 Cylinders, 20 H. P., 96 Inch Wheel Base, $850

The Willys-Overland Company 125 Central Avenue TOLEDO, OHIO

Willys "Sleeve Valves"

For years Willys-Overland manufactured cars using the popular Knight Sleeve Valve engine (right), unique in that it had no valves, springs, or camshaft. Instead two simple sleeves in each cylinder moved silently up and down on a film of oil. Directly below: The Willys-Knight Country Club model, 1924, with a sleeve-valve en-gine. The 1923 ad at bottom, right, boasted "distinguished" Willys-Knight touring cars (five passengers) for $1,235, three-passenger road-sters for the same price, and five-passenger sedans for $1,795. One of the Willys-Knight slogans throughout the years was "The Engine Improves with Use." They felt they could make this claim because no valve grinding was re-quired and the engine actually seemed to operate better after a few thousand miles.

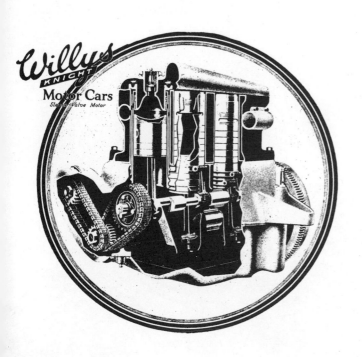

Pack More Pleasure Into Your Life!

DISTINGUISHED alike for its beauty, com-fort and extraordinary performance, the new Willys-Knight has rightfully earned its great place in public esteem.

Underneath the custom features of coachwork is the marvelous Willys-Knight sleeve-valve engine—the same type of engine that powers many of the most famous hand-built cars of Europe.

The Willys-Knight sleeve-valve engine actually improves with use. Performance is even quieter and more powerful at ten thousand miles than at five hundred. Carbon only makes it better; and there is no valve grinding.

Many owners report 50,000 miles and more without any engine adjustment.

WILLYS-OVERLAND, INC., TOLEDO, OHIO
Willys-Overland Ltd., Toronto, Ont.

WILLYS-KNIGHT

TOURING 5-pass., $1235   ROADSTER 3-pass., $1235   SEDAN 5-pass., $1795   COUPE-SEDAN 5-pass., $1595
TOURING 7-pass., $1435   SEDAN 7-pass., $1995   ALL PRICES F. O. B. TOLEDO

THE ENGINE IMPROVES WITH USE

Like many other automobile companies, Willys-Overland got into the low-priced-car field early and in 1928 it added a small car called the Whippet to the Willys-Knight line. While still proclaiming the advantages of the patented Knight Sleeve Valve engine, the company offered the Whippet Coach (left background) at $625, a bargain in 1928. The first Whippet cars were four-cylinder models made to compete with Ford and Chevrolet. Willys reduced the prices of these cars continually—in 1927 the Whippet Roadster was selling at $455—but he never succeeded in taking the inexpensive-car market away from Ford and Chevrolet. His margin of profit was so small that it is a question whether the Whippet ever profited Willys-Overland very much.

Later a six-cylinder Whippet was manufactured. At bottom is the 1929 Willys-Knight two-door close-coupled Sedan or Club Coupé. This car was designed by Amos Northrupp.

Index